D0369664

Poetry Workbook

Eric Boagey
Head of English, Eastfields High School, Merton

University Tutorial Press

Published by University Tutorial Press Ltd
842 Yeovil Road, Slough SL1 4JQ

All rights reserved. No portion of this book may be reproduced by
any process without written permission of the publishers

© E J Boagey 1977

ISBN 0 7231 0748 3

Published 1977
Reprinted (with minor corrections) June 1978
Reprinted December 1978
Reprinted 1979, 1981

Printed in Great Britain by
Spottiswoode Ballantyne Ltd,
Colchester and London

ACKNOWLEDGEMENTS

The author is indebted to the following for permission to use copyright material:
George Mackay Brown for *The Storm* and, with The Hogarth Press Ltd, for *Hamnavoe Market* from *The Year of the Whale* by George Mackay Brown.
R H Blyth for *Haiku* published by Hokuseido.
Carcanet New Press Ltd for *Still-Life.* Copyright Elizabeth Daryush 1976 from *Collected Poems* (Carcanet, Manchester).
Chatto & Windus Ltd for *Visiting Hour* and *Starlings* by Norman MacCaig from *Rings on a Tree* and for *The Tomb of David Hume* by Alan Bold from *A Perpetual Motion Machine.*
The Cresset Press (Barrie & Jenkins) for *Call Not to Me* by Ruth Pitter from *Collected Poems 1926-1966.*
J M Dent & Sons Ltd and the Trustees for the Copyrights of the late Dylan Thomas for *Ears in the Turrets Hear* by Dylan Thomas from *Collected Poems 1934-52.*
André Deutsch Ltd for *Sunken Evening* and *The Edge of Day* by Laurie Lee from *My Many Coated Man.*
Faber & Faber Ltd for *Who's Who* by W H Auden from *Collected Shorter Poems; The Old Gumbie Cat* by T S Eliot from *Old Possum's Book of Practical Cats; Considering the Snail* by Thom Gunn from *My Sad Captains; Trout* by Seamus Heaney from *Death of a Naturalist; Thistles* and *Skylarks* by Ted Hughes from *Wodwo.*
Hamish Hamilton Ltd for *The day God gave thee, Ring-a-Ring o'neutrons* and *Mary, Mary* by Paul Dehn from *Quake, Quake, Quake.* Copyright © 1961 by Paul Dehn, Hamish Hamilton Ltd, London.
Rupert Hart-Davis/Granada Publishing Ltd for *The Labourer* from *Song at the Year's Turning* and *To a Young Poet* from *The Bread of Truth* by R S Thomas.
William Heinemann Ltd for an extract from *Breathless* from *South Col* by Wilfred Noyce.
Katz, Leavy, Rosensweig & Sindle and Mrs Edgar Lee Masters for *The Hill* by Edgar Lee Masters.
Hope Leresche and Sayle for *40-Love, Dreampoem* and *A Square Dance.* © 1967 Roger McGough from *Penguin Modern Poets 10.*
Lund Humphries Publishers Ltd for *This Winter Pond* by Ai' Ching from *Poems of Solitude* translated by Jerome Ch'en and Michael Bullock.

MacGibbon & Kee Ltd/Granada Publishing Ltd for *Grasshopper* and *ygUDuh* by E E Cummings from *Complete Poems*.

Alasdair Maclean for *Among Ourselves* from *Poetry Introduction 2* published by Faber & Faber Ltd.

London Magazine Editions for *Silence* and *grow show blow flow* by Eugen Gomringer and *Near the Guernsey Coast* by Dom Sylvester Houedar from *Concrete Poetry: An International Anthology*, ed. Stephen Bann.

The New Statesman for *The Hero* by Roger Woddis.

Wilfred Owen's Literary Estate and Chatto & Windus Ltd for *Send-Off, Futility* and *The Last Laugh* from *Collected Poems* by Wilfred Owen edited by C. Day Lewis.

Maeve Peake for *Victoria Station 6.58 p.m.* by Mervyn Peake from *Selected Poems*.

Penguin Books Ltd for an extract from *The Battle of Maldon* and from *Beowulf* from *The Earliest English Poetry* translated by Michael Alexander *(Penguin Modern Classics 1966)* pp.114—5, 49. Copyright © Michael Alexander 1966.

Laurence Pollinger Ltd and the Estate of the late Mrs Frieda Lawrence for *At the Window, Discord in Childhood, The Blue Jay* and *Mountain Lion* from *The Complete Works of D H Lawrence* published by William Heinemann Ltd.

Carl Sandburg for *Jazz Fantasia* from *Smoke and Steel*, published by Harcourt Brace Jovanovich, Inc., reprinted by permission of the publishers.

Sidgwick & Jackson Ltd for *Tunisian Patrol* from *Collected Poems of Richard Spender*. Copyright by Richard Spender 1945.

A P Watt & Son and Robert Graves for *Counting the Beats* by Robert Graves.

A P Watt & Son and The National Trust for *Boots* from *The Definitive Edition of Rudyard Kipling's verse*.

A P Watt & Son, M B Yeats, Miss Anne Yeats and the Macmillan Co. of London and Basingstoke for *The Second Coming* and *The Song of Wandering Aengus* from *The Collected Poems of W B Yeats*.

The publishers have been unsuccessful in seeking permission to reproduce *Reflection* from *The Carpentered Hen and Other Tame Creatures* by John Updike. They ask the author or his agent to contact them about this should this book succeed in coming into their hands.

CONTENTS

PREFACE

Dylan Thomas refers to his poetry as 'my craft or sullen art' and in doing so places the emphasis on the technique which the poet employs to express his meaning. This book is concerned with poetic technique, though not to the exclusion of every other aspect of poetry. The study of style and verse form, however, is an enormous one and the chapters that follow are not intended to be exhaustive of their particular subjects; they are more an introduction to the analysis of poetry for students who are approaching it for the first time. The assumption is that the poet is a conscious craftsman, shaping the phrase, the line and the stanza according to certain aesthetic principles and that the student of poetry is entering more completely into the world of the poet when he can recognise the technique behind the inspiration and the craftsman behind the thinker. The book's epigraph, therefore, might be: it is the art of the artist to hide his art and the art of the critic to find it again.

The chapters in the book are devoted to single topics. A brief introduction with illustrative examples is followed by a poem or a group of poems on which questions are asked in order to develop a fuller understanding of the topic being studied. There is a selection of poems for closer study — some of them linked directly to the work in the chapters — and a number of general questions, similar to those that appear in examination papers, in order to bring the poems together under various themes and forms.

If the book is used on a weekly basis it will provide a course lasting about half the school year. It gives students the examples they need to identify a characteristic trait of poetic style or a particular form of verse, and it establishes the vocabulary that is needed to write about poetry with critical precision. I hope it will also lead to a greater awareness of the poet's use of language, to a sense of the continuing development of English poetry from the early alliterative verse to the innovations of our own day and to a realisation that the poet's fundamental task is to put his craft or his art at the service of his meaning.

THE POETRY WE USE

You don't have to look far to find poetry in everyday speech. It is
there all the time, part of the language we use from early
childhood onwards, helping us to express ourselves in a lively and
imaginative way. We don't call it poetry, of course, and we
certainly don't associate it with the poetry we read in school, yet
this special way of expressing ourselves contains many of the
characteristics we recognise as belonging to poetry, such as
rhythm, rhyme and a colourful use of words. These occur in our
speech quite naturally and we use the language of poetry without
knowing it. If we look, therefore, at some of the expressions that
are commonly used in spoken English, we shall see that they have
some connection with the poetry we read in books.

There are many common sayings which crept into our
language at some time in the past and which mean more than they
say. For instance, to 'make hay while the sun shines' doesn't apply
only to farmers, for we can see that the meaning can be
transferred to situations other than making hay. Similarly,
everyone can 'make a mountain out of a molehill' without being a
magician. A person can:

> be a wolf in sheep's clothing
> have too many irons in the fire
> have pins and needles
> have his head in the clouds
> be up a gum tree

We very easily recognise that these sayings are not to be taken
literally, in an exact sense. They are expressed in the imaginative
language we find in poetry. Some of these common sayings are
proverbs:

> Every cloud has a silver lining.
> It never rains but it pours.
> It's a long road that has no turning.
> A bird in the hand is worth two in the bush.

In many of them, one phrase balances another and produces a
rhythm which comes easily off the tongue:

> Out of sight, out of mind.
> Set a thief to catch a thief.
> Least said, soonest mended.
> In for a penny, in for a pound.

Occasionally there is a rhyme:

> Ne'er cast a clout till May is out.
> A cleft chin, the devil within.
> An apple a day keeps the doctor away.
> Finders keepers, losers weepers.

In English folklore there is a whole wealth of short rhyming verses which are used when the occasion arises:

> Early to bed,
> Early to rise,
> Makes a man healthy,
> Wealthy and wise.

> Red sky at night,
> Shepherds' delight
> Red sky at morning,
> Shepherds' warning.

> Ladybird, ladybird, fly away home,
> Your house is on fire and your children have gone.

Our first acquaintance with poetry probably comes through nursery rhymes, with their simple, bold rhythms, regular rhymes and miniature narratives. Later, in streets and playgrounds, we shout or chant verses and jingles to accompany games, to select the person who is 'it', to make jokes, to call people names, to tease and torment, and to mark special days in the year, such as birthdays, Christmas, Easter and Guy Fawkes Day. We have probably all heard or used variations on:

> Ip dip sky blue,
> Who's it, not you.
> Not because you're dirty,
> Not because you're clean,
> Not because your mother said
> You're the fairy queen.

> Remember, remember,
> The fifth of November,
> Gunpowder, treason and plot.
> I see no reason
> Why gunpowder treason
> Should ever be forgot.

> Rain, rain, go away,
> Come back another day!

> It's raining, it's pouring,
> The old man's snoring.

> Ask no questions,
> You'll get no lies.
> Keep your mouth shut,
> You'll get no flies.

These sayings, proverbs, verses and rhymes — and many more like them — are part and parcel of our ordinary language and their popularity and continued vitality prove that there is something basically enjoyable about the sound of poetry: the lines may go with a swing, the rhymes may be clever and witty, the ideas can be wild and nonsensical or simple and wise, and the occasions on which they can be introduced into play and conversation are endless. We accept all this without question; it's when we meet poems on the printed page that the problems begin! Yet the professional poet is not introducing anything new — he is simply arranging his material in a more deliberate shape, searching for a more expressive language and finding his subjects in a wider range of ideas and experience.

Before embarking on the study of this kind of poetry, however, you could make your own collection of 'the poetry we use' by taking up some of the following suggestions and questions:

1. What examples can you find of the imaginative use of language in everyday speech? Are there any common sayings, popular proverbs or even slang expressions which seem to you to show a lively and poetic use of words?

2. Can you quote any proverbs that rhyme, or that have a balanced rhythm?

3. What rhymes, verses or songs can you remember from your own schooldays? Can you collect some examples from generations older and younger than your own?

4. Try to find out:

the rhyme that is used for remembering a spelling rule;

the verse that helps you to remember the number of days in each month;

the verse that names the Sundays in Lent;

a rhyme for what is customarily eaten on Good Friday;

a chant used by supporters at a football match.

5. In and around London you might hear someone speak of his feet as 'me plates of meat' or his eyes as his 'mince pies'. He might 'take a butcher's' (butcher's hook — look) and put on his 'titfer' (tit-for-tat — hat). It is cockney rhyming slang, still being used to add a touch of humour to conversation. Can you find some more examples of it?

6. Advertisements are a new source of catchy poetry, from the famous 'drinka pinta milka day' and 'Beanz Meanz Heinz' to the jingles that one hears on commercial television and radio. Collect some examples of advertising verse and of advertising language that has a deliberately poetic touch about it.

METRE

I'm sorry if this line is longer
Than this one,
But I was out when the man came to check
The metre.

When you look at the printed page of a book you can usually tell
at a glance whether what you are looking at is a poem or a piece of
prose. You know by the shape of the print on the page. If it makes
a solid block with most of the lines running to the margin, you
know that it is prose; if it is arranged in verses or if it runs
continuously down the centre of the page, you guess that it is
poetry.

What gives poetry its shape on the page? There is not one
single answer, but we can say that most poetry gets its shape from
the length of the lines and the way the lines are arranged in verses;
and the length of the line is determined by the number of stresses,
or beats, which the line contains. If a poet decides, therefore, that
he will write a verse containing lines of four stresses, he is
regulating the length of the lines and he is creating the shape we
recognise as 'poetry'. If the first line contains four stresses and the
second line two stresses, then his shape will again be different. But
shape itself is not the poet's aim. He is more interested in the
pattern of stresses that creates the shape, for this pattern of sound
gives the poem its rhythm.

There is nothing new or unusual about stresses in language, of
course: we are using them in our speech all the time. If you say 'I
hate doing housework', you will find yourself stressing the words
hate and *house;* if you say 'yesterday and today', you will stress
the first syllable of 'yesterday' and the second syllable of 'today'.
In fact, no matter what you say, you are going to stress some
syllables more than others. The poet makes use of this speech
habit by creating a pattern of stressed and unstressed syllables in
his verse. This pattern, which forms the basic rhythm of the poem,
is known as the *metre.* Here is a simple example:

When fírst my wáy to fáir I tóok,
Few pence in púrse had Í,
And lóng I úsed to stánd and lóok
At thíngs I cóuld not búy.

The metre in this verse is 4 3 4 3 and because the language is very

4

simple the stresses fall on complete words, though they can fall on single syllables in words also. This 4 3 4 3 metre is often used in the composition of ballads and hymns because it is springy and tuneful. It is known as *ballad metre* and is one of several basic metrical patterns which are used in English poetry. Because metres can create a special effect in verse, the poet chooses the metre best suited to the mood and meaning he wants to convey. A witches' spell, for instance, might be written in a regular, repetitive, fast-moving metre to give a concentrated and hypnotic effect; and in this speech from *Macbeth* Shakespeare uses a metre of four stresses throughout:

> Double, double toil and trouble;
> Fire burn and cauldron bubble.
> Fillet of a fenny snake,
> In the cauldron boil and bake;
> Eye of newt, and toe of frog,
> Wool of bat, and tongue of dog,
> Adder's fork, and blind-worm's sting,
> Lizard's leg, and howlet's wing,
> For a charm of powerful trouble,
> Like a hell-broth boil and bubble.
> Double, double toil and trouble;
> Fire burn and cauldron bubble.

Often a metre can give a physical effect. In *Breathless* Wilfred Noyce describes what it feels like to climb a mountain and he uses a metre of two stresses to a line to suggest the breathlessness of the climber:

> Heart aches,
> Lungs pant
> The dry air
> Sorry, scant.
> Legs lift
> And why at all?
> Loose drift,
> Heavy fall.

In contrast, Alfred Noyes suggests vigorous movement in *The Highwayman* by varying the stresses from six to two:

> The wind was a torrent of darkness among the gusty trees,
> The moon was a ghostly galleon tossed upon cloudy seas,
> The road was a ribbon of moonlight over the purple moor,
> And a highwayman came riding —

Riding — riding
A highwayman came riding, up to the old inn door.

Metre first of all gives order to a poem by establishing a basic pattern. It also helps to hold the attention of the listener or reader who gets used to the pattern of sound and knows what to expect. It might also connect with the fact that everybody enjoys a simple rhythm. Why else do we tap our feet and our fingers when we hear a regular beat in music, clap in time and dance rhythmically? Is it possible that it can have something to do with our regular bodily rhythms, like inhaling and exhaling and the beating of the heart?

For reference
When there is one stress to a line (rather rare), the line is said to be a *monometer;* two stresses: *dimeter;* three stresses: *trimeter;* four stresses: *tetrameter;* five stresses: *pentameter;* six stresses: *hexameter;* seven stresses: *heptameter;* eight stresses: *octameter.*

Most English poetry that is written in metrical form is based on a combination of stresses and syllables. There is not only a regular pattern of stresses, but a regular pattern of syllables also. Thus, if you look at the ballad stanza with its 4 3 4 3 metre, you will discover that the number of syllables in each line is 8 6 8 6. In the witches' chant the syllable count is 7 or 8 to a line. This linking-up of stress and syllable count is known as *stress-syllable verse.* When there is no recognisable pattern of stress, but a clear pattern of syllables, the verse is called *syllabic verse.* Read the following poems and answer the questions on them:

1.   A wonderful bird is the pelican;
His beak can hold more than his belican.
He can take in his beak
Enough food for a week.
I'm damned if I know how the helican.

a)   What pattern of syllables is made in the lines?
b)   How many stresses to each line?

2.   There was a young man of Japan,
Whose limericks never would scan.
When they said it was so,
He replied, "Yes, I know,
But I always try to get as many words into the last line as
ever I possibly can."

a)   Where is the joke in this limerick?
b)   What does the word ' scan ' mean?

3.   From *Nightmare*, by W S Gilbert.

For your brain is on fire — the bedclothes conspire of your
     usual slumber to plunder you:
First your counterpane goes, and uncovers your toes, and
     your sheet slips demurely from under you;
Then the blanketing tickles — you feel like mixed pickles —
     so terribly sharp is the pricking,
And you're hot and you're cross, and you tumble and toss till
     there's nothing 'twixt you and the ticking.
Then the bedclothes all creep to the ground in a heap and
     you pick 'em all up in a tangle;
Next your pillow resigns and politely declines to remain at its
     usual angle!
Well, you get some repose in the form of a doze, with hot
     eyeballs and head ever aching,
But your slumbering teems with such horrible dreams that
     you'd very much better be waking.

a)   What metre is the poem written in?
b)   Why do you think W S Gilbert chose this metre when
       writing about a nightmare?
c)   Is the syllabic pattern regular?

4.   *Considering the Snail*

The snail pushes through a green
night, for the grass is heavy
with water and meets over
the bright path he makes, where rain
has darkened the earth's dark. He
moves in a wood of desire,

pale antlers barely stirring
as he hunts. I cannot tell
what power is at work, drenched there
with purpose, knowing nothing.
What is a snail's fury? All
I think is that if later

I parted the blades above
the tunnel and saw the thin
trail of broken white across
litter, I would never have
imagined the slow passion
to that deliberate progress.

Thom Gunn

a) Is there a recognisable metre in this poem?
b) Is there a pattern of syllables?
c) Is it, therefore, stress-syllable or syllabic verse?
d) What exactly is the 'wood' that the snail moves in?
e) What purpose has the snail in moving across the litter?
f) What aspect of the snail is Thom Gunn most interested in?

5. Read also *Counting the Beats* by Robert Graves (page 101) and answer the questions on the poem.

METRICAL FEET

Take the word 'unzip'. It has two syllables: un-zip. When you say it, which syllable do you stress, the first or the second? If we use the sign ° to signify the unstressed syllable and the sign ´ to denote a stressed syllable, then we can indicate the way we say *unzip* by writing ùnzíp. Try this with other words:

> *enjoy   picnic   referee   pyramid*

Write down the words, divide them into syllables and indicate by using the two signs which are the stressed and which the unstressed syllables. Your answer should be:

> ènjóy   pícnìc   rèfèrée   pýràmìd

When you look at the stress pattern that has been made, you will see that *picnic* (´°) is the reverse of *enjoy* (°´) and *pyramid* (´°°) is the reverse of *referee* (° °´). These words can be taken as examples of the four main rhythmic units in English verse — or, to speak technically, of the four main metrical feet. Each foot has a name:

enjoy	°´	the iambus	a rising rhythm of two syllables
picnic	´°	the trochee	a falling rhythm of two syllables
referee	°°´	the anapaest	a rising rhythm of three syllables
pyramid	´°°	the dactyl	a falling rhythm of three syllables

The syllables going to make up these metrical feet do not have to be in the same word, of course. In a line of verse they can fall upon separate words, so that a phrase like *I am* can be iambic, *stop it* can be trochaic, *on the hill* can be an anapaest and *sing to me* can be a dactyl. It might help you to remember which foot is which by saying to yourself:

> I am (iambus) (°´) tro-chee (´°) an-a-paest (°°´) dac-tyl-ic (´°°)

Before going on to the use of metrical feet in poetry, get some practice at recognising the four main feet. Write down the following words and phrases, divide them into syllables, put in the stress marks and say what the pattern of sound is. In the phrases, the word to be stressed is in italics:

> Awake   Ada   beautiful   is the *east*   person   on the *run*
> chaos   crackpot   *why* do you   alone   dignified
> autumn   by the *hand*   remote   burning   impure
> barbarous   my *lord*   design   *hail* to thee

It may be difficult to believe that a poet can write verse which uses these metrical feet so precisely that they form a rhythmical pattern of sound, yet this is so. Look at the following examples:

Sweet day, so cool, so calm, so bright,   o′ o′ o′ o′
The bridal of the earth and sky   o′ o′ o′ o′

It forms a pattern of four iambic feet to each line.

Tiger! Tiger! burning bright   ′o ′o ′o ′
In the forests of the night   ′o ′o ′o ′

Three full trochees in each line; the fourth trochee lacks the unstressed syllable and could be called half a foot!

Like the leaves of the forest when   oo′ oo′ oo′ oo′
    summer is green,
That host with their banners at sunset   o′ oo′ oo′ oo′
    were seen.

Four complete anapaests in the first line, but an unstressed syllable missing from the anapaest at the beginning of the second line.

Take her up tenderly,   ′oo ′oo
Lift her with care,   ′oo ′
Fashioned so slenderly   ′oo ′oo
Young and so rare.   ′oo ′

A pattern of dactyls, with the second foot in lines two and four missing the unstressed syllables.

As you can see from the missing feet in the examples above, not many poets stick rigidly to a metrical pattern. If they did, their verse would be mechanical in rhythm and rather monotonous. Variations are used to produce a sound that is nearer to the rhythms of the spoken voice; for in English it is the number of stresses to a line that is significant, not the regularity of the feet that make up the stresses. It is not necessary for the appreciation of a poem, therefore, to be able to account for every foot in a line, but it can help one to appreciate the poet's craft to be able to trace the predominant rhythmic unit and to see whether it adds to the total effect of the poem. The simplicity of the two-syllable feet, with their cadences so close to a natural speech, creates a different impression on a listener from the more musical three-syllable feet. However, before looking at some examples of metrical feet in action, remember that:

i)   a foot consists of one stressed syllable, together with the unstressed syllables that attach themselves to it;

ii) it is rare to find an absolutely regular pattern of metrical feet, but there is usually a predominant foot forming the basic pattern;

iii) opinions may differ on how a particular line should be divided into feet;

iv) the metrical shape of a poem tends to be obscured or even changed when the poem is read aloud.

1. The following lines are taken from *Night Mail* by W H Auden, a poem describing the journey of a train from London to Glasgow.

This is the night mail crossing the
    border,
Bringing the cheque and the postal
    order,
Letters for the rich, letters for the poor,
The shop at the corner and the girl next
    door.

a) The first line consists of: dactyl, trochee, dactyl, trochee. Work out the pattern of the remaining lines.

b) What effect do you think Auden is aiming at in using these rhythms?

2. The quality of mercy is not strain'd,
It droppeth as the gentle rain from heaven
Upon the place beneath: it is twice bless'd;

a) What metrical foot is being used? Why is this foot used so much in poetic drama?

b) There is an irregularity in *twice bless'd*. What effect has it?

3. O young Lochinvar has come out of the west,
Through all the wide border his steed was the best.

a) Omitting the first two syllables of each line, which belong to an incomplete foot, what metrical foot is used in the remainder of the lines?

b) What makes this foot suitable for a lively story of action and romance?

4. When he killed the Mudjokivis,
Of the skin he made him mittens,
Made them with the fur side inside,
Made them with the skin side outside,
He, to get the warm side inside,
Put the inside skin side outside;
He, to get the cold side outside,

Put the warm side fur side inside,
That's why he put fur side inside,
Why he put the skin side outside,
Why he turned them inside outside.

a) The author is mimicking the style of a serious poem called
Hiawatha, by Longfellow. What metrical foot is used
throughout? Is it perfectly regular?

b) What is your opinion of the tick-tock rhythm? How does it
influence the way the poem is read and the way we react to it?

5. *The Old Gumbie Cat*

I have a Gumbie Cat in mind, her name is Jennyanydots;
Her coat is of the tabby kind, with tiger stripes and leopard
spots.
All day she sits upon the stair or on the step or on the mat:
She sits and sits and sits and sits — and that's what makes a
Gumbie Cat!

But when the day's hustle and bustle is done,
Then the Gumbie Cat's work is but hardly begun.
And when all the family's in bed and asleep,
She slips down the stairs to the basement to creep.
She is deeply concerned with the ways of the mice —
Their behaviour's not good and their manners not nice;
So when she has got them all lined up on the matting,
She teaches them music, crocheting and tatting.

I have a Gumbie Cat in mind, her name is Jennyanydots;
Her equal would be hard to find, she likes the warm and
sunny spots.
All day she sits beside the hearth or in the sun or on my hat:
She sits and sits and sits and sits — and that's what makes a
Gumbie Cat!

But when the day's hustle and bustle is done,
Then the Gumbie Cat's work is but hardly begun.
As she finds that the mice will not ever keep quiet,
She is sure it is due to irregular diet
And believing that nothing is done without trying,
She sets straight to work with her baking and frying.
She makes them a mouse-cake of bread and dried peas,
And a beautiful fry of lean bacon and cheese.

I have a Gumbie Cat in mind, her name is Jennyanydots;
The curtain-cord she likes to wind, and tie it into
sailor-knots.

She sits upon the window-sill, or anything that's smooth and
    flat:
She sits and sits and sits and sits — and that's what makes a
    Gumbie Cat!

But when the day's hustle and bustle is done,
Then the Gumbie Cat's work is but hardly begun.
She thinks that the cockroaches just need employment
To prevent them from idle and wanton destroyment.
So she's formed, from that lot of disorderly louts,
A troop of well-disciplined boy-scouts,
With a purpose in life and a good deed to do —
And she's even created a Beetles' Tattoo.

So for Old Gumbie Cats let us now give three cheers —
On whom well-ordered households depend, it appears.

T S Eliot

a)   Eliot uses alternating 4-line and 8-line stanzas. What metrical
     foot is used in each of these stanzas?
b)   What connection is there between the habits of the Gumbie
     Cat and the two kinds of metrical feet used in the poem?
c)   Understanding the metrical structure of a poem can help in
     reading it aloud correctly. Write out the following complete
     lines and indicate, by putting in stress marks, how they should
     be read: lines 4 6 24 31 38.

For reference
Spondee: two stressed syllables, such as in *ámén, twíce bléss'd;*
caesura: a pause within a line, as in *upon the place beneath: it is*
twice bless'd; **enjambment:** a run-on line when the meaning is
carried over to the next line without pause; **end-stopped line:**
when there is a pause at the end of a line.

RHYME

Ask a person what makes poetry different from 'ordinary' writing and you can bet he'll say, "Well, poetry rhymes". Where does the idea that 'poetry rhymes' come from? Probably that time in a child's life when he is first introduced to nursery rhymes; and the idea sticks, perhaps because, of all the things that go to make up poetry, rhyme is the most easily recognisable. It might also be the most enjoyable, for there is something pleasant about the sound of words echoing one another at more or less regular intervals. In addition to the pleasant sound, however, the use of rhyme is an example of the poet searching for a pattern which will give shape and order to the meaning the words themselves express. I think rhyme also helps to catch your attention, to help you listen, as you wonder how the poet will manage his next one. Used awkwardly or with obvious contrivance rhyme can spoil a poem, but where there is a perfect matching of word with meaning the rhyme can give a poem style and impact.

Rhyme has a long history in English literature, from Anglo-Saxon times onwards, and there were periods, such as the eighteenth century, when rhyme reached peaks of brilliance in poetry; yet English is not a language that lends itself easily to rhyme, as some languages do. The trouble is in the endings of words. It has been estimated that the average number of words to an ending is three, which doesn't give a poet much choice. Some words rhyme with only one other word (*mountain — fountain*) and some words cannot be rhymed at all (*circle, breadth, desert, monarch, month, virtue, wisdom,* for instance). Not surprisingly, English poets have looked for alternatives to rhyme, and in the 20th century rhyme has become of comparatively minor importance in poetry. Some poets have given it up altogether because it gets in the way of free expression; or they have taken to a modified type of rhyme in which the identical sounds are not so obvious; and one poet actually invents words in order to create his rhymes.

Before going on to the use of rhyme in poetry, however, we ought first to establish what ordinary rhyme is and to look at some of the variations on it. Here are some words which we would all recognise as rhymes:

still — fill   roam — home   strong — long   dart — heart

You will notice that:

i)   vowel sounds are identical in rhymed words;

14

ii) the consonants that follow the rhymed vowels are the same;
iii) the consonants that precede the rhymed vowels are not the same.

When the rhyming words are monosyllables (as those above) and when the rhyme falls on the stressed syllable at the end of words containing more than one syllable, the rhyme is said to be a *masculine* rhyme:

> *confess — express   conspire — desire   respect — collect*
> *lake — mistake*

If the rhyme is on two syllables, a stressed syllable followed by an unstressed one, (identical in the two words) the rhyme is *feminine* or *double:*

> *walking — talking   solemn — column   porter — daughter*
> *brightly — tightly*

Rhymes on three syllables, often in separate words, are not very common and are called *triple* rhymes:

> *tenderly — slenderly   spoken one — broken one*
> *tournaments — ornaments*

All these are 'perfect' rhymes. There are 'imperfect' rhymes also which don't correspond completely and it is these rhymes that are often used by twentieth-century poets. There is *assonance*, when the vowels agree but the consonants don't:

> *soon — mood   heap — need   design — reside*
> *hive — time   curl — turn*

There is *consonance*, when the final consonants only agree:

> *match — hitch   strike — hawk   pale — mile   years — pours*

There is *pararhyme*, when both consonants agree, but the vowel does not:

> *groined — groaned   sipped — supped   mystery — mastery*
> *sweets — sweats*

There is *unstressed rhyme*, when the rhyming syllable is unstressed:

> *wonder — liver   brothers — flowers   dancing — walking*

And there is *eye-rhyme*, when the words look alike but are pronounced differently (though they may have rhymed at some time in the past):

rough — bough   mind — wind   quay — day   go — do
love — move

1. Now study the following lists of words. Pick out the perfect
rhymes in each group, saying whether they are masculine,
feminine or triple. Then find an example of assonance from
group *a*, consonance from group *e* and eye-rhyme from group *f*.

a)   green   growth   seem   seen
b)   greeting   heaving   breathing   seething
c)   proved   shoved   showed   moved
d)   speedily   greedily   readily   heedlessly
e)   boozer   snoozes   loses   blazer
f)   enough   bough   laugh   sow

Part of the art of rhymed verse is to produce a regular
structure of rhyme throughout the poem, serving to separate one
verse from another and occasionally to provide a linking thread
between verses. This is known as the *rhyme scheme* and it can be
worked out by giving the same letter of the alphabet to all the
line-endings that rhyme:

Oh some have killed in angry love
And some have killed in hate,
And some have killed in foreign lands
To serve the business state,
The hangman's hands are abstract hands
Though sudden death they bring.
"The hangman keeps our country pure,"
Says Harry Fat the King.

The rhyme scheme of this poem is calculated by calling *love* 'a',
hate 'b', and *lands* 'c'. When you reach *state*, however, you find
that it rhymes with *hate*. It therefore has the same letter, 'b'.
Hands rhymes with *lands* and is 'c'. *Bring* doesn't rhyme with
anything so far and therefore becomes 'd'. *Pure* is also unrhymed
and becomes 'e'. *King* rhymes with *bring* and is therefore 'd'. The
rhyme scheme in full can be written: a b c b c d e d and the
pattern that the poet has created to give the poem a framework of
related sounds can easily be seen. Rhyme schemes apply only to
terminal rhymes — that is, those that appear at the end of lines.
But rhyme can turn up in the middle of lines, hence *medial* or
internal rhyme, and even at the beginning of lines, when it is called
initial rhyme.

Wilfred Owen, one of the great poets of the First World War,
used traditional rhyme in his poetry, but was also the first poet

writing in English to use consonance and pararhyme as part of a rhyme scheme. It is appropriate, therefore, to study both traditional and modern forms of rhyme in his poetry. The first poem, *The Send-Off* describes a company of soldiers boarding a train at a lonely country railway station on the first stage of their journey to the front line in France. The second poem, *Futility*, expresses Wilfred Owen's feelings about the death of an individual soldier and the senseless waste of life that accompanies war. Both poems were written a few months before the poet himself was killed in battle.

2.   *The Send-Off*

Down the close darkening lanes they sang their way
To the siding-shed,
And lined the train with faces grimly gay.

Their breasts were stuck all white with wreath and spray
As men's are, dead.

Dull porters watched them, and a casual tramp
Stood staring hard,
Sorry to miss them from the upland camp.

Then, unmoved, signals nodded, and a lamp
Winked to the guard.

So secretly, like wrongs hushed-up, they went.
They were not ours:
We never heard to which front these were sent.

Nor there if they yet mock what women meant
Who gave them flowers.

Shall they return to beatings of great bells
In wild train-loads?
A few, a few, too few for drums and yells,

May creep back, silent, to still village wells
Up half-known roads.

a)   Write out the rhyme scheme. How does it link the 3-line and the 2-line verses?
b)   Does the rhyme scheme correspond to the division of the subject of the poem? Give a title to each of the four sections.
c)   Why should the faces of the men be *grimly gay*?
d)   What is being suggested by the wreath and spray on the men's breasts?

e)   Is there anything in the description of the signals and the lamp which seems to be connected with line 11?

f)   What is the effect of the repetition of: *A few, a few, too few . . . ?*

g)   Why should the roads be *half-known?*

3.   *Futility*

Move him into the sun —
Gently its touch awoke him once,
At home, whispering of fields unsown.
Always it woke him, even in France,
Until this morning and this snow.
If anything might rouse him now
The kind old sun will know.

Think how it wakes the seeds, -
Woke, once,the clays of a cold star.
Are limbs, so dear-achieved, are sides,
Full-nerved, — still warm, — too hard to stir?
Was it for this the clay grew tall?
— O what made fatuous sunbeams toil
To break earth's sleep at all?

a)   Trace the pattern of rhyme and pararhyme in the poem.

b)   Where is there an example of i) consonance; ii) assonance?

c)   Do the final rhymes in each stanza give an effect of completeness, like clicking the thought into place, or do they seem forced and obvious?

d)   How does Wilfred Owen give the impression that he is writing spontaneously, in the midst of the situation?

e)   In what way did the sun wake *the clays of a cold star?*

f)   What is the poet asking in the first question in the poem?

g)   What does *this* refer to in line 12?

h)   What contrast in feeling is there in the two stanzas?

i)   What is the point of the title *Futility?*

EARLY ENGLISH POETRY

When the Anglo-Saxons invaded Britain in the 5th century after
the departure of the Romans, they brought with them, and
continued to develop, a body of oral poetry which had as its
subject the history and legends of the Germanic tribes from whom
they were descended. The poetry was recited or sung in the halls
of the Anglo-Saxon lords by bards who accompanied themselves
on the harp. The bard recited the poems from memory, but he
would introduce his own variations into the stories and there were
never two recitations of a poem that were exactly the same,
though the main events would be faithfully described. The role of
the bard was not merely to entertain the earl and his company
after a meal; he was also a means of uniting the people by relating
deeds from their common past, he was the 'voice and memory of
the tribe', for in those days there were none of the media which
we have now to tell the people of the events of the world and to
form their attitude towards them. Much — perhaps most — of this
oral poetry has been lost; but some heroic poems, as well as poetry
on Christian themes which was being composed during these
centuries before the Conquest, were eventually written down,
probably by monks, and these have been miraculously preserved
for over a thousand years — the oldest vernacular literature in
Western Europe.

What makes the poetry of the Anglo-Saxon period interesting
from a technical point of view is that it was based upon a special
metrical system. We have seen in an earlier workpaper that
traditional English poety is stress-syllable verse, in which the metre
combines a count of stresses and syllables in a line. In
Anglo-Saxon poetry, however, stress alone was important and the
number of syllables in a line could vary from eight to twenty —
they weren't counted at all. Each line of the poem would contain
four stresses, two on either side of a pause which usually occurred
somewhere near the middle of the line and which was probably
marked by the bard's striking a chord on the harp. The bard's skill
did not end there, however, for in addition to maintaining a
four-stress line it had to include an alliterative pattern that was
anything but easy. The key to the alliteration was the initial letter
of the first stress after the pause. One of the stresses in the first
half of the line must alliterate with this and the other one may,
though this was not essential. The last stress in the line must not

alliterate at all. Michael Alexander, in *The Earliest English Poems*, writes this of Anglo-Saxon alliterative verse:

> It is a formalised version of the rhythm of emphatic speech, derived originally from the rhythm of the heart and the rhythm of the breath. Reduced to its crudest form, it might be expressed by

> BANG ... BANG : BANG ... CRASH

Look now at an example of the verse. The following lines describe the voyage of a boat over the sea to Denmark and they are a translation from the original Anglo-Saxon:

> Away she went over a wavy ocean,
> boat like a bird, breaking seas,
> wind-whetted, white-throated,
> till curved prow had ploughed so far
> — the sun standing right on the second day —
> that they might see land loom on the skyline,
> then the shimmer of cliffs, sheer moors behind,
> reaching capes.
>   The crossing was at an end.

Study, first, where the stresses come in each line. You might agree that they fall on these words or parts of words:

> Away   went   wavy   ocean
> boat   bird   break   seas
> wind   whet   white   throat
> curved   prow   ploughed   far
> sun   stand   sec   day
> see   land   loom   sky
> shimmer   cliffs   sheer   moors
> reach   capes   cross   end

Assuming that the pause in the first line comes after *went*, then the alliteration will be based on the third stress, which is *wavy*. The stresses in the first half-line, *away* and *went*, alliterate with it, whilst the fourth stress, *ocean*, doesn't alliterate at all. It is a line that conforms strictly to the rules of Anglo-Saxon metre. Look at the alliteration in the remaining lines and decide whether it is perfectly regular or whether it varies from the model.

1.   Anglo-Saxon alliterative verse is illustrated at greater length in an extract from *The Battle of Maldon*, one of the great early English poems.

In 911 the Danes raided England with ninety-three ships and
ravaged the towns of Folkestone, Sandwich and Ipswich.
Eventually they reached Maldon in Essex and made a base on
the island of Northey in the estuary of the River Blackwater.
Northey Island was linked to the mainland by a causeway
eighty yards long and eight feet wide. The Vikings asked for
tribute from the English, but it was refused. When the tide
went out the Vikings attempted to cross the causeway, but
they presented an easy target for the waiting Saxons and in a
gesture of generosity (or perhaps over-confidence)
Bryhtnoth, the Saxon earl, allowed the Vikings to cross the
causeway without harm and to re-form their ranks on the
mainland. The battle began. Bryhtnoth was slain, many of his
followers fled, but the earl's personal retinue, demonstrating
their loyalty to their lord, fought on to the end.

The extract is from the early part of the poem in which a Viking
spokesman tries to strike a bargain with Bryhtnoth; if he pays a
tribute the Danes will call off their attack. Bryhtnoth refuses.

Then Bryhtnoth dressed his band of warriors,
from horseback taught each man his task,
where he should stand, how keep his station.
He bade them brace their linden-boards aright,
fast in finger-grip, and to fear not.
Then when his folk was fairly ranked
Bryhtnoth alighted where he loved best to be
and was held most at heart — among hearth-companions.

Then stood on strand and called out sternly
A Viking spokesman. He made speech —
threat in his throat, threw across the seamen's
errand to the Earl where he stood on our shore.

'The swift-striking seafarers send me to thee,
bid me to say that thou send for thy safety
rings, bracelets. Better for you
that you stay straightaway our onslaught with tribute
than that we should share bitter strife.
We need not meet if you can meet our needs:
for a gold tribute a truce is struck.

Art captain here: if thou tak'st this course,
art willing to pay thy people's ransom,
wilt render to Vikings what they think right,
buying our peace at our price,

we shall with that tribute turn back to ship,
fare out on the flood, and hold you as friends.'

Bryhtnoth spoke. He raised shield-board,
shook the slim ash-spear, shaped his words.
Stiff with anger, he gave him answer:

'Hearest 'ou, seaman, what this folk sayeth?
Spears shall be all the tribute they send you,
viper-stained spears and the swords of forebears,
such a haul of harness as shall hardly profit you.

Spokesman for scavengers, go speak this back again,
bear your tribe a bitterer tale:
that there stands here 'mid his men not the meanest of
    Earls,
pledged to fight in this land's defence,
the land of Aethelred, my liege lord,
its soil, its folk. In this fight the heathen
shall fall. It would be a shame for your trouble
if you should with our silver away to ship
without fight offered. It is a fair step hither:
you have come a long way into our land.

But English silver is not so softly won:
first iron and edge shall make arbitrement,
harsh war-trial, ere we yield tribute.'

a) Trace the pattern of stresses and alliteration in the first seven
     lines of the Viking spokesman's speech. What irregularities are
     there?
b) Remembering that alliterative verse was intended to be recited
     to an audience, what qualities, in your opinion, does it have?
c) In what sense is the word *dressed* used in line 1?
d) What do you understand by *linden-boards* and
     hearth-companions?
e) What is particularly interesting about line 20?
f) What tribute did the Vikings demand and what did they
     promise to do if it was paid?
g) Where do you detect a note of arrogance in the Viking's
     speech?
h) What *tribute* was Bryhtnoth willing to pay?
i) What do you take to be the meaning of the following phrases?
     i)   *viper-stained spears;*
     ii) *swords of our forebears;*
     iii) *iron and edge shall make arbitrement.*

j) Why should Bryhtnoth call the Vikings *scavengers?*

k) The Anglo-Saxons often spoke in what are called 'understatements'. Which phrase, used by Bryhtnoth to describe himself, has the characteristic modesty of an understatement?

l) What impression do you get of Bryhtnoth's character as a leader from the first stanza of this extract?

m) What tone of voice do you think would be used by Bryhtnoth for the following statement:

> . . . . *It would be a shame for your trouble*
> *if you should with our silver away to ship*
> *without fight offered.*

n) Where in the extract is there an expression of strong patriotic feeling?

2. Read also the extract from *Beowulf* (page 124).

SIMILE

He eats like a horse
You're daft as a brush!
The meat was as tough as old boots.
I slept like a log

Our language is full of comparisons — strange, unexpected, amusing, vivid comparisons that make conversation or a piece of writing more colourful and more easily understood. They are part of the common currency of speech and many of them have a long history, having originated, most probably, in the mind of a person who was something of a poet himself. These comparisons, usually introduced by 'like' or 'as', are called *similes* and they constitute an important part of the poet's literary style. In poetry they are not all that easy to write. I doubt if a poet could produce a good simile by sitting down and trying to think one up. They tend to come by what is sometimes called 'inspiration' — by allowing a part of the mind to be open to an imaginative association that seems to arrive without a conscious striving for it — as much of the language of poetry seems to arrive.

Chaucer was one of the first English poets to use simile, for before him, during the Old English period, the simile was not frequently used. Chaucer's similes tend to be short, simple ones that make one specific comparison. In the General Prologue to *The Canterbury Tales*, for instance, he describes the Prioress as having 'eyes as grey as glass' and the Monk's horse as being 'brown as a berry'. The Miller had a wart on his nose from which grew a tuft of hairs 'red as the bristles of a sow's ears'. The Friar's eyes twinkled in his head 'as do the stars on a frosty night'. This type of simile occurs in poetry of all periods and styles. It is an apt comparison between the object or person being described and something similar to it in one particular. The only point of comparison between the Friar's eyes and the star is that they both twinkle: the other characteristics of the star, such as its remoteness, its size, or its age, are not used at all. We see from this simile, however, how a poet can introduce a new visual element into his poetry, giving it a further dimension. The picture of the remote twinkling star presented to a reader's mind through the comparison keeps his mind alert, attracts his attention and provides an enjoyment that the plain statement cannot give.

Though the individual simile can be very striking, a chain of connected similes throughout a poem can have even more impact.

Wilfred Owen, in a war poem called *Dulce et Decorum Est* describes the horrific experience of retreating from the front line during a gas attack. He opens the poem with two similes:

Bent double, like old beggars under sacks,
Knock-kneed, coughing like hags, we cursed through sludge

He goes on to describe the plight of a soldier who, unable to put on his gas mask in time, stumbles and flounders 'like a man in fire or lime' until he is overcome by the fumes and, in a convulsive agony, is flung into a wagon, his eyes writhing in a face that was 'like a devil's sick of sin'. At every jolt of the wagon the blood comes gargling from his lungs:

Obscene as cancer, bitter as the cud
Of vile incurable sores on innocent tongues

and with this inescapable memory of the horrors of war, Owen asks that children should not be taught the old 'lie' that it is glorious to die for one's native land. Much of the force of the poem lies in these similes — beggars, hags, fire, devil, cancer, incurable sores — each one of which is strong and charged with feeling. They are the poet's means of emphasising his disgust at the obscenities of war and they provide an emotional theme to the poem.

In *How Beastly the Bourgeois Is* D H Lawrence also uses a series of connected similes which take in, not one, but several points of comparison so that they become extended throughout the poem. Lawrence is expressing his dislike of a certain type of upper-middle-class Englishman who, though handsome and healthy, has no guts, and if faced with a little 'moral difficulty' would go 'soggy, like a wet meringue' and turn into a fool or a bully. Lawrence sees this beastly specimen of the bourgeois

Nicely groomed, like a mushroom
standing there so sleek and erect and eyeable —
and like a fungus, living on the remains of bygone life
sucking his life out of the dead leaves of greater life than his
    own.

And even so, he's stale, he's been there too long.
Touch him, and you'll find he's all gone inside
just like an old mushroom all wormy inside, and hollow
under a smooth skin and an upright appearance
Full of seething, wormy, hollow feelings
rather nasty —

and he ends by wishing that all these obnoxious types could be kicked over 'like sickening toadstools' and allowed to melt back into the soil of England. It is rather a sour poem, but Lawrence makes brilliant use of the fungus, mushroom, toadstool similes to carry his ridicule and scorn of the bourgeois throughout the poem.

Similes can also become descriptive passages in their own right, adding to the pictorial effect as well as offering an apt comparison. In *Morte d' Arthur* Tennyson describes the barge that carries the dying Arthur across the water in terms of a swan:

> So said he, and the barge with oar and sail
> Moved from the brink, like some full-breasted swan
> That, fluting a wild carol ere her death,
> Ruffles her pure cold plume, and takes the flood
> With swarthy webs.

There is much more here than is strictly needed for a comparison with the departing barge, but the description itself is beautiful and it includes details, such as the swan's song, which Tennyson brings in by way of appropriate association with the dying Arthur.

These are some of the uses of simile in poetry — to make a simple comparison, to appeal to our imagination, to reinforce the poet's meaning, to add a pictorial element and to create associations. There are other uses — particularly the simile that describes what cannot be described except by comparing it with something else, but each simile needs to be looked at separately and evaluated for its contribution to the effectiveness of the poem as a whole.

1.   Below are some quotations containing similes. Say which of them in your opinion was written: to express disgust; to convey a sense of perspective; to provide an association with character; to suggest mystery and power; to create a comic effect; to suggest regal grandeur; to imply a mood of depression; to express a delicacy of feeling.

a)   Mr and Mrs Floyd, the cocklers, are sleeping as quiet as death, side by wrinkled side, toothless, salt and brown, like two old kippers in a box.

b)   It flows through old hushed Egypt and its sands, Like some grave mighty thought threading a dream.

c)   Far off, like floating seeds, the ships Diverge on urgent voluntary errands.

d)   The barge she sat in, like a burnish'd throne, Burn'd on the water

e) Wings like bits of umbrella.
Bats!
Creatures that hang themselves upside down like an old rag to
    sleep
f) You make me feel like
Sunday night at the village hall
baby
g) Like the pearl of dew
On the grass in my garden
In the evening shadows,
I shall be no more.
h) There was Dai Puw. He was no good.
They put him in the fields to dock swedes,
And took the knife from him, when he came home
At late evening with a grin
Like the slash of a knife on his face.

2. *Herder's Song*

My bull is as white as the silvery fish in the river; as white as
    the egret on the river bank; as white as new milk.
His bellowing is like the roar of the Turk's cannon from the
    great river.
My bull is dark as the rain-cloud, that comes with the storm.
He is like Summer and Winter; half of him dark as the
    thundercloud; half of him as white as sunshine.
His hump shines like the morning star.
His forehead is as red as the ground hornbill's wattles,
His forehead is like a banner, seen by the people from afar.
He is like the rainbow.
I shall water him at the river, and drive
My enemies from the water with my spear.
Let them water their cattle at the well;
The river for me and my bull.
Drink, O Bull, of the river. Am I not here with
My spear to protect you?

Translated from a Sudanese song.

a) Why do you think the herder chose to express his feelings
about his bull in similes?
b) From what subjects are the similes drawn?
c) Describe factually what the bull looked like. What difference is
there between a literal description and the song of the herder?

3.   *This Winter Pond*

This winter pond —
Lonely like an old man's heart
That has savoured all human sadness;
This winter pond —
Dry and sunken like an old man's eyes
That have lost their lustre through hard labour;
This winter pond —
Desolate, like an old man's hair
That is sparse, grey and frosted;
This winter pond —
Sullen like a sad old man
Who shrivels up under the sullen sky.

Ai Ch'ing

a) Which words in the poem describe the pond itself?
b) What is the real subject of the poem — the pond or an old
    man?
c) Do you think the connected similes are used effectively in this
    poem?

4. In certain long narrative poems the simile is not just a phrase,
but a whole descriptive passage in its own right. The following
example of this 'epic' simile is from *Sohrab and Rustum*, by
Matthew Arnold (1822-88). Rustum, the famous, ageing champion
of the Persians, is about to fight Sohrab, the young Tartar
champion.

And Rustum to the Persian front advanc'd,
And Sohrab arm'd in Haman's tent, and came.
And as afield the reapers cut a swathe
Down through the middle of a rich man's corn,
And on each side are squares of standing corn,
And in the midst a stubble, short and bare;
So on each side were squares of men, with spears
Bristling, and in the midst the open sand.
And Rustum came upon the sand, and cast
His eyes towards the Tartar tents, and saw
Sohrab come forth, and ey'd him as he came.
As some rich woman, on a winter's morn,
Eyes through her silken curtains the poor drudge
Who with numb blacken'd fingers makes her fire —
At cock-crow, on a starlit winter's morn,

When the frost flowers the whiten'd window panes —
And wonders how she lives, and what the thoughts
Of that poor drudge may be; so Rustum ey'd
The unknown adventurous Youth, who from afar
Came seeking Rustum, and defying forth
All the most valiant chiefs; long he perus'd
His spirited air, and wonder'd who he was.
For very young he seem'd, tenderly rear'd;
Like some young cypress, tall, and dark, and straight,
Which in a queen's secluded garden throws
Its slight dark shadow on the moonlit turf,
By midnight, to a bubbling fountain's sound —
So slender Sohrab seem'd, so softly rear'd.
And a deep pity enter'd Rustum's soul
As he beheld him coming; and he stood
And beckon'd to him with his hand . . ..

a) Where does each epic simile begin and end?
b) How appropriate is the second simile? Is there anything you
would criticise in it?
c) What impression of Sohrab is Matthew Arnold giving in the
third simile?
d) Write i) a justification and ii) a criticism of these epic similes.

For a further example of simile, read the extracts from *Morte
d'Arthur* (page 106) and *Skylarks* (page 107) and answer the
questions on them.

METAPHOR

She's got green fingers.
He said he wasn't going to play second fiddle.
He's so pig-headed about things.
The business ran out of steam.

Our everyday speech is full of expressions which don't mean what they say. After all, her fingers aren't exactly green, he doesn't really play a fiddle, his head is not, of course, like a pig's, and the business wasn't powered by steam in the first place. No, the expressions are not meant to be taken literally, in a plain, matter-of-fact sense; they are *metaphors* and they are to be understood metaphorically.

The metaphor, like the simile, is based upon a point of similarity between two things; but whereas the simile states that one thing is *like* another, the metaphor identifies them completely. Thus, 'the child chattered *like a monkey*' is a simile, but 'that child *is a perfect monkey*' is a metaphor. We cannot say literally of the child that he *is* a monkey, because he is not — he is a human being. We can, however, use the same word in a literal and a metaphorical (or figurative) sense. We could say that the soldier was literally *dying of his wounds*, but only figuratively speaking that he was *dying of boredom* (though even that might just be possible!).

Metaphors in common use are drawn from every sphere of life imaginable — sport, the theatre, animals, trades, occupations, the sea, the countryside, the law, religion — and they are evidence of the continuing vitality of our language. We can speak, for instance, of a person who is *big-headed, bull-necked, tight-fisted, hamstrung, warm-hearted, cold-blooded, catty, sheepish, shrewish;* we can *get down to brass tacks, have an axe to grind, jump out of the frying pan into the fire, fly off the handle, get bogged down, be in the soup, on the carpet, under the weather, in a stew, out on a limb, in an ivory tower, up to the eyes in work, down in the mouth, round the bend, in a pickle;* we can *burn the midnight oil, be sold a pup, smell a rat, do a fiddle, cough up money, lead someone a dance, pay through the nose, get our backs up, keep the flag flying, eat humble pie, be sent to Coventry, lend a hand, foot a bill, catch the Speaker's eye, be on tenterhooks, cut off our nose to spite our face . . .* there is no end to metaphorical expressions in English! They keep the language lively and they testify to the richness of invention and imagination that has been at work over centuries of linguistic development.

It is hardly surprising, therefore, that metaphor plays a large part in the language of poetry, though the poet tends to create his own metaphors rather than draw upon those that are already in use. The functions of common and poetic metaphor, however, are not fundamentally different; for just as a figurative phrase in everyday speech can express a meaning more directly and strikingly than a literal statement can, so a metaphor in poetry can illuminate a thought, reach into the imagination and enable us to perceive a meaning more directly than its literal equivalent is able to do. Its purpose is not unlike that of the simile: it helps the poet to express an attitude towards his subject, it catches the eye and the ear, it draws upon word-pictures to present an idea in a concrete form, it speaks directly from feeling to feeling, often bypassing the intellect, and it can provide a connecting thread throughout a poem which gives a sense of unity.

Shakespeare is one of the masters of metaphor and he uses it to great effect in all his writings. In one of his sonnets, for instance, he uses the seasons as a metaphor for age. It is a common-enough idea to see youth as spring and old age as winter, but Shakespeare gives it a resonance beyond the single point of comparison and allows the associations of his metaphor to play upon the mind of his reader:

> That time of year thou mayst in me behold
> When yellow leaves, or none, or few, do hang
> Upon those boughs which shake against the cold,
> Bare ruin'd choirs, where late the sweet birds sang.

What has Shakespeare made of this commonplace metaphor? He has given a picture of late autumn that implies more about age than mere advancing years.

Yellow leaves, or none, or few conveys a sense of barrenness, a mood of desolation . . . *boughs which shake against the cold* makes one feel the pain, the weakness and the comfortlessness of age, the coming of winter and perhaps death . . . *the bare ruin'd choirs* (the choir stalls) implying loneliness, with *ruin'd* having a special force, suggesting, perhaps, that there has been some moral decay at work in his life . . . *where late the sweet birds sang* is a reminder of youth and happiness. The extended metaphor has created a vivid word-picture that contains a number of subtle associations from which we, subconsciously perhaps, piece together an impression of an ageing man.

A different metaphorical effect is produced by the following passage from *Othello*. Othello has killed his wife, Desdemona, only to learn that she was innocent of the infidelity of which he accused her. He turns his condemnation upon himself and, in a passionate outburst over her dead body, exclaims:

> O cursed, cursed slave! whip me ye devils
> From the possession of this heavenly sight!
> Blow me about in winds! roast me in sulphur!
> Wash me in steep-down gulfs of liquid fire! —
> O Desdemon! dead! Desdemon! dead! O!

Is it possible to make a literal rendering of this speech? What would be left if the concrete, elemental images of Othello's cry for his own damnation were removed and literal expression substituted? Very little of the passion, probably, and even less of the drama.

1.   A succession of related metaphors running through a speech can be seen in the following quotation from *Macbeth*. Macbeth has just received news of the death of his wife and he reflects on the passage of time and on the meaning — or meaninglessness — of life. Read the lines and then answer the questions that follow them.

> She should have died hereafter;
> There would have been a time for such a word.
> Tomorrow, and tomorrow, and tomorrow,
> Creeps in this petty pace from day to day,
> To the last syllable of recorded time;
> And all our yesterdays have lighted fools
> The way to dusty death. Out, out, brief candle!
> Life's but a walking shadow, a poor player
> That struts and frets his hour upon the stage,
> And then is heard no more; it is a tale
> Told by an idiot, full of sound and fury,
> Signifying nothing.

a)   How many references to the stage are there in the lines?
b)   What metaphorical phrase suggests the slow passage of time?
c)   Which two metaphors imply that life is comparatively short?
d)   Quote the expressions which convey these characteristics of man: his pride and his self-pity; his foolishness; his self-importance; his lack of meaning.

2. *Thistles*

> Against the rubber tongues of cows and the hoeing hands of
>   men
> Thistles spike the summer air
> Or crackle open under a blue-black pressure.
>
> Every one a revengeful burst
> Of resurrection, a grasped fistful
> Of splintered weapons and Icelandic frost thrust up
>
> From the underground stain of a decayed Viking.
> They are like pale hair and the gutturals of dialects.
> Every one manages a plume of blood.
>
> Then they grow grey, like men.
> Mown down, it is a feud. Their sons appear,
> Stiff with weapons, fighting back over the same ground.

Ted Hughes

a) The metaphor of fighting predominates in this poem,
reinforcing the idea that thistles are tough, aggressive, persistent
plants. Make a list of words in the poem that are used
metaphorically to convey the idea of aggression.
b) What seems to you appropriate about thistles growing *from
the underground stain of a decayed Viking?*
c) There are two places in the poem where the poet expresses
through metaphor what in literal English would be that no
matter how often you cut down thistles, they always reappear.
Quote these phrases.

3. *Trout*

> Hangs, a fat gun-barrel,
> deep under arched bridges
> or slips like butter down
> the throat of the river.
>
> From depths smooth-skinned as plums
> his muzzle gets bull's eye;
> picks off grass-seed and moths
> that vanish, torpedoed.
>
> Where water unravels
> over gravel beds he
> is fired from the shallows
> white belly reporting

flat; darts like a tracer-
bullet back between stones
and is never burnt out.
A volley of cold blood

Ramrodding the current.

Seamus Heaney

a) The first metaphor likens the trout to a *fat gun-barrel* as it
hovers in the deep water under the bridges. As you go through
the poem you begin to realise that the poet is deliberately
choosing metaphors to fit a theme which characterises the
trout. What are these metaphors and what idea is common to
them?

b) Which point of view do you take: that the metaphors are
overdone and distort the description of the trout; or that they
are skilful and imaginative and bring out the true nature of the
fish?

4. Read also: *The Labourer* (page 102), *Sunken Evening*
page (103), *Edge of the Day* (page 104) and *Ears in the Turrets
Hear* (page 105) and answer the questions on the poems.

PERSONIFICATION

And there goes the bell for the third month
and Winter comes out of its corner looking groggy
Spring leads with a left to the head
followed by a sharp right to the body

Roger McGough's poem, *Fight of the Year,* uses an old technique
of poetry in a new way. He writes about spring and winter as
though they were people — boxers, in fact, fighting it out as the
year gets under way until winter gives in to spring. To write about
something that is obviously not human as though it were a person
is to use a figure of speech known as *personification.* It has a long
history. The ancient Greeks and Romans were using
personification when they created their mythical gods and
goddesses to represent forces in nature and in man: Neptune was
the personification of the ocean, Aurora of the dawn, Bacchus of
wine-drinking, Cupid of love and the nine muses the
personifications of the arts and sciences who 'inspired' poets and
scientists in their creative endeavours. In medieval drama the
psychology of man was depicted in personifications that included
devils, angels and the seven deadly sins — Sloth, Gluttony, Envy,
Lust and Co. When these abstract emotions were presented as
persons, the audience was given a picture of itself that it could
easily identify with and understand. Today we are more concerned
with the individual and feel that dramatised abstractions lack the
realism that we expect from drama. The grand personifications, in
fact, are not very evident in the contemporary world, though we
are occasionally reminded of them in such figures as Old Father
Time, the statue of Liberty, the blindfold figure of Justice and in
that noble lady who once 'ruled the waves'.

Personification was popular in poetry in the middle ages, when
poets used it to convey a religious or moral message, and during
the Renaissance when the influence of classical learning was very
strong. It could be used for a variety of effects and had a visual
element that gave a concreteness to abstract themes. John Donne
— the Elizabethan poet — in bed with his mistress and objecting to
being disturbed by the morning sun begins his poem with a lively
and amusing personification:

Busy old fool, unruly Sun,
Why dost thou thus,
Through windows and through curtains call on us?

By doing so he immediately creates a mood of impatience and disdain which gives us an important first impression of the speaker.

In a later, more serious poem, Donne opens with:

Death, be not proud, though some have called thee
Mighty and dreadful, for thou art not so

and he uses the personification of death as a means of facing his own death and as an argument against death's invincibility.

Poets of later centuries have also made the creation of personifications part of their technique and it is not difficult to find clever or touching cameos such as: 'Laughter, holding both his sides'. . . 'wrinkled care'. . . 'moping melancholy and moon-struck madness'. . . 'pure-eyed Faith and white-handed Hope'. . . 'Death and his brother, Sleep'. . . 'the still small voice of gratitude'. There was a tendency amongst certain poets, however, often minor, less-gifted ones, to overdo personification and to make it seem forced, stilted and even pompous. The modern reader is turned off poetry when he comes across an accretion of personification that is combined with an artificial poetic diction:

Fair laughs the morn, and oft the zephyr blows,
While proudly riding o'er the azure realm
In gallant trim the gilded vessel goes;
Youth on the prow and Pleasure at the helm;

And with verse as heavy-going and ornate as this, personification with a capital letter went out of fashion.

There remains, however, a type of personification which is an integral part of poetic style and which is frequently used by contemporary poets. This is simply to write about inanimate objects — as opposed to abstractions — as though they had human feelings: 'a weeping mist'. . . 'the mournful word the seas say'. . . 'shrieking iron'. . . 'drinking the sea and eating the rock/a tree struggles to make leaves'. . . 'hearing the stones cry out under the horizon'. . . 'the mowing machine ate at the field of grass'. . . The poet is not creating an independent figure but using a metaphor and choosing his point of comparison from the human world. It is sometimes difficult to draw a line strictly between true personification and the personalised metaphor (the latter has been called 'animation'), but whatever name we give to it, this figure of speech obviously helps the poet to express himself more effectively, for human life can provide a vast range of metaphor with which to suggest the sights and sounds and movements of the inanimate world. The danger is, of course, that the 'human' touch will become sentimental or exaggerated and instead of accepting the metaphor we shall be subconsciously muttering "but a mist can't weep . . . stones don't cry out . . . mowing machines don't eat . . . " and when this happens the poetic technique is beginning to fail.

1. Read the following poem, by P B Shelley, and answer the questions on it:

> Art thou pale for weariness
> Of climbing heaven, and gazing on the earth,
> Wandering companionless
> Among the stars that have a different birth —
> And ever changing, like a joyless eye,
> That finds no object worth its constancy?

a) What is being personified in the poem?
b) If Shelley has put into his personification something of his own character, what sort of person would he be?
c) Answer the question the poem asks.

2. *Tunisian Patrol*

> The Night lies with her body crookedly flung
> In agony across the sharp hills;
> By the fitful moon her nostrils are taut, quivering;
> She is tensed in cold sweat and lonely fear,
> Giving sudden birth in dark, sly, trodden places
> To her unlawful issue, blind, hideous Death.
>
> Across the pain-jerked body of the Night
> We must go, taking the new-born Death in arms,
> Holding it close, warmly to us, as our own,
> Giving it new games to play, new toys to tear apart.

Richard Spender

a) Look carefully at the personification of Night. Why has the poet given Night this particular character?
b) In what way can Night have *unlawful issue?*
c) Can you see a double meaning in the word *arms?*
d) Put into your own words what the poet is saying in the last two lines.

3. *At the Window*

> The pine-trees bend to listen to the autumn wind as it
>   mutters

Something which sets the black poplars ashake with
  hysterical laughter;
As slowly the house of day is closing its eastern shutters.

Farther down the valley the clustered tombstones recede,
Winding about their dimness the mist's grey cerements, after
The street-lamps in the twilight have suddenly started to
  bleed.

The leaves fly over the window, and utter a word as they pass
To the face that gazes outwards, watching for night to waft a
Meaning or a message over the window glass.

D H Lawrence

a) Point out the personifications in the poem.
b) Why has Lawrence chosen these particular personifications? Is
    there a connection between them and the face gazing out of
    the window, looking for a meaning or a message?
c) Why is *cerements* an appropriate metaphor to apply to the
    mist around the tombstones?
d) Express the meaning of the third line in a more literal style.
e) Which words and phrases help to create the sombre mood of
    the poem?
f) What question are you left with after reading this poem?

4. *Love's Philosophy*

The fountains mingle with the river
And the rivers with the ocean,
The winds of heaven mix forever
With a sweet emotion;
Nothing in the world is single,
All things by a law divine
In one another's being mingle —
Why not I with thine?

See the mountains kiss high heaven
And the waves clasp one another;
No sister-flower would be forgiven
If it disdain'd its brother;
And the sunlight clasps the earth,
And the moonbeams kiss the sea —
What are all these kissings worth,
If thou kiss not me?

P B Shelley

a) Make a list of the personifications in the poem.
b) Express briefly, in your own words, the argument behind the 'philosophy'.
c) What do you think of the argument? Are you convinced by it or not?
d) If the argument is not convincing, does it mean that the poem is without meaning?

5. Read and study: *The Last Laugh* by Wilfred Owen (page 110) and answer the questions on the poem.

SYMBOL

Among Ourselves is a poem by Alasdair Maclean describing a little
domestic scene in which the mother knits, the father reads and the
son smokes a cigarette:

> Among ourselves we rarely speak.
> Our tongues are thick with custom.
> Inside our house, at this time of the year,
> there's only the ticking of the clock
> and the click of my mother's needles
> as she knits herself away from where
> she cast on. My father's pages rustle.
> He makes himself a nest of newspaper.
> I sit in a corner, smoking. Every time
> I draw on my cigarette I hear
> the tiny hiss of tobacco becoming ash.

It is a simple poem, effectively describing the boredom and the
impatience of the young man at being cooped up with parents
who have settled down to a life of domestic stagnation. What
clinches the portrait of the son is the last sentence of the poem:

> . . . . *Every time*
> *I draw on my cigarette I hear*
> *the tiny hiss of tobacco becoming ash.*

If we take this to mean exactly what it says and nothing more we
understand that the son is smoking a cigarette which, quite
naturally, is turning to ash. There's nothing unusual about that.
But the detail can be taken to mean something more than this; the
'tobacco becoming ash' stands for the young man's life, for in that
claustrophobic situation at home his life is being burned up,
wasted, as the tobacco is being burned up and turned into ash. The
cigarette has been used therefore as a symbol of the young man's
wasted life. It is a small factual detail that represents an idea. The
interesting thing about the symbol is that we are not told what it
means. We, the readers, have to put two and two together and
work out the meaning.

The word *symbol* is related to the Greek word *symbolon*,
which was a half-coin carried away by each of the two parties to
an agreement as a pledge of their good faith. A symbol, therefore,
is like half a coin — it is an object; the other half of the coin is the
idea it represents. When a person understands the symbol the two

parts come together and the meaning is passed on. When the symbol is not recognised, then it remains no more than an object. A cross would mean nothing to a pagan because he is unaware of its symbolic significance; to a Christian, however, it could act as a reminder of his faith, uniting him with the idea. Everything depends on the two parts coming together.

There is a vast reservoir of traditional symbols used in everyday life which the average person recognises and easily comprehends. White, for instance, is taken as a symbol of purity, purple of royalty; the crown is a symbol of kingship, the gold ring of the union of marriage, the lion of strength, the dove of peace and the tree is a symbol of life itself. In fact, most of the common natural phenomena, such as the sun, the moon, water, fire, mountains, rivers and rocks, as well as domestic objects such as bread, wine, salt and fruit can be used as symbols, though exactly what they symbolise is not constant and varies with the context. The symbols, you will notice, are all concrete — we can see them, they have shape; the thing that is symbolised is not concrete; it is an abstraction, an idea.

In poetry the symbol should be understood from the poem itself, though some poets have created a private symbolism which, without a key, remains obscure and difficult to interpret. A successful symbol in a poem is one which is able to convey a meaning to the reader directly, either because it is conventionally accepted or because it has been prepared for in the poem itself. The poet uses a symbol because it gives his idea a concrete shape which, without explanation, unites the understanding of the reader with the mind of the poet.

1. *Victoria Station. 6.58 p.m.*

    Sudden, beneath the pendant clock arose
    Out of the drab and artificial ground
    A horse with wings of scarlet, and pale flowers
    Glimmered upon its forehead, while around

    His neck and mane like wreaths of incense streamed
    Young hosts of stars, and as his eyes burned proud,
    The men with black umbrellas stood and stared
    And nudged each other and then laughed aloud.

    Mervyn Peake

a) The symbol in this poem is a horse, but it is not an ordinary horse. What is exceptional about it?
b) What details of the poem are intended as a contrast to the horse?

c) The men with black umbrellas laugh at the horse. What criticism of them is the poet making?

d) Mervyn Peake was a gifted artist and an imaginative poet and novelist — quite the opposite of a city businessman. How can this give us a clue to understanding the symbolism of the poem?

2. *Dreampoem*

> in a corner of my bedroom
>> grew a tree
>> a happytree
>> my own tree
> its leaves were soft
>> like flesh
> and its birds sang poems for me
> then
>> without warning
> two men
>> with understanding smiles
> and axes
>> made out of forged excuses
> came and chopped it down
> either yesterday
>> or the day before
> i think it was the day before

Roger McGough

a) We are told enough about the tree to realise that it symbolises the poet's way of life. What was characteristic of his way of life?

b) What impression do you get of the men who chopped down the tree?

c) What fear is behind the dream of the arrival of the two men?

d) How is the dream-state suggested in the final lines of the poem?

3. *Go, lovely Rose!*

> Go, lovely Rose!
> Tell her, that wastes her time and me,
>> That now she knows,
> When I resemble her to thee,
> How sweet and fair she seems to be.

Tell her that's young
And shuns to have her graces spied,
   That hadst thou sprung
In deserts, where no men abide,
Thou must have uncommended died.

   Small is the worth
Of beauty from the light retired;
   Bid her come forth,
Suffer herself to be desired,
And not blush so to be admired.

   Then die! that she
The common fate of all things rare
   May read in thee:
How small a part of time they share
That are so wondrous sweet and fair.

Edmund Waller

a) Here the young lover sends a rose to the girl he loves, but he
   intends it to be seen as a symbol, not merely as a pretty flower
   and in the first verse the rose is *sweet and fair*, as the girl is.
   What other meaning is the rose given in the remainder of the
   poem?
b) Express as clearly as you can what the lover is complaining of.
c) What impression do you get of the girl?
d) Describe the diction of the poem.

4.   *The Poison Tree*

I was angry with my friend:
I told my wrath, my wrath did end.
I was angry with my foe:
I told it not, my wrath did grow.

And I watered it in fears,
Night and morning with my tears;
And I sunned it with smiles,
And with soft deceitful wiles.

And it grew both day and night,
Till it bore an apple bright.
And my foe beheld it shine,
And he knew that it was mine.

And into my garden he stole
When the night had veiled the pole:
In the morning glad I see
My foe outstretched beneath the tree.

William Blake

a)   The tree is here a symbol of man's hate and begins to grow
because anger is not honestly expressed. How does the tree
continue to grow?

b)   Without explaining the symbolism of the apple, say how the
foe is killed.

5.   *The Second Coming*

Turning and turning in the widening gyre
The falcon cannot hear the falconer;
Things fall apart; the centre cannot hold;
Mere anarchy is loosed upon the world,
The blood-dimmed tide is loosed, and everywhere
The ceremony of innocence is drowned;
The best lack all conviction, while the worst
Are full of passionate intensity.

Surely some revelation is at hand;
Surely the Second Coming is at hand.
The Second Coming! Hardly are those words out
When a vast image out of *Spiritus Mundi*
Troubles my sight; somewhere in sands of the desert
A shape with lion body and the head of a man,
A gaze blank and pitiless as the sun,
Is moving its slow thighs, while all about it
Reel shadows of the indignant desert birds.
The darkness drops again; but now I know
That twenty centuries of stony sleep
Were vexed to nightmare by a rocking cradle,
And what rough beast, its hour come round at last,
Slouches towards Bethlehem to be born?

W B Yeats

a)   The poem was published in 1921 and is a prophecy of the
political evils that were to culminate in the Second World War.
The Second Coming is not of Christ, but of the symbolic
rough beast. Which lines in the first stanza imply that political
order is breaking down?

b)   What is suggested about these new forces in the world by:
       A shape with lion body and the head of a man,
       A gaze blank and pitiless as the sun,
c)   Can you say what the *indignant desert birds* might represent?
d)   In your opinion, has Yeats created an effective symbol in this poem?

ALLITERATION

Alliteration might be described as the poetic equivalent of the
tongue-twister, for both get their effect from a repetition of
sound. Tongue-twisters like *sixteen standard twin-screw steel
cruisers* and *round the rugged rock the ragged rascal ran* or *red
leather, yellow leather* or *still the sinking steamer sank* soon make
one trip up, with their repetition of consonants, but everyone
seems to enjoy trying to say them and their popularity suggests
that there is something deep in us that is intrigued by alliterative
sound. Young children fall easily into the habit of repeating
sounds such as 'ma-ma' and 'da-da' and, at the other extreme,
politicians can add to the emotional impact of a speech by
introducing an apt alliterative phrase ('I have nothing to offer but
blood, toil, tears and sweat'). Alliteration also appears in spells,
oaths and advertisements, perhaps because the repetition of a
sound can suggest a mysterious or mystical meaning and have a
mesmerising effect on those who hear it. Most of all, it is an
age-old part of the poet's technique and it has been used to create
a wide range of interesting poetic effects.

Perhaps the most common use of alliteration in poetry is to
create a pattern of harmony — like identical notes in music — and
to call attention to certain words that the poet wants to
emphasise. When Robert Burns writes:

> My heart's in the highlands, my heart is not here,
> My heart's in the highlands a-chasing the deer

he is repeating the 'h' sound to give it emphasis, perhaps because
the repeated 'h' suggests the sighing and the longing that are the
theme of the poem.

Samuel Coleridge, in *The Rime of the Ancient Mariner*, wrote:

> The fair breeze blew, the white foam flew,
> The furrow followed free;
> We were the first that ever burst
> Into that silent sea.

The main alliteration is on the 'f' sound, but there is minor
alliteration on the 'b' and 's' also. The repetition of the 'f' gives a
harmony and a unity to the lines, but it also seems to suggest the
continuous movement of the wind and the water.

Alliteration can help to produce a rhythmic beat, as in these
lines describing the army of Don John of Austria on the march:

Strong gongs groaning as the guns boom far,
Don John of Austria is going to the war,
Stiff flags straining in the night-blasts cold,
In the gloom black-purple, in the glint old-gold,
Torchlight crimson on the copper kettle-drums,
Then the tuckets, then the trumpets, then the cannon, and he
comes.

Here there is not only alliteration in short phrases and in single lines, but also a theme of connected sounds throughout the passage, creating together a tightly-knit alliterative scheme that reinforces the vigour and splendour of the advancing army.

If it is overdone, however, alliteration can ruin a poem. It is easily recognised by the reader and it can equally easily be seen as an artificial adornment to a poem, calling in question the poet's sincerity. On the other hand, one should try not to find alliteration that is not there, since not every string of words beginning with the same letter occurs deliberately. If you say, 'Sam's going to the sea-scouts on Sunday' you are certainly repeating the 's' sound, but you're not exactly a poet. You are not doing it for harmony, or emphasis, or pattern or to show off your verbal technique — it just happens! We need to distinguish, therefore, between accidental and intentional alliteration in poetry.

1.   Read the following quotations and consider the use of alliteration in each one:

a)   In Xanadu did Kubla Khan
       A stately pleasure dome decree:
       Where Alph, the sacred river, ran
       Through caverns measureless to man
       Down to a sunless sea.

b)   Shall I part my hair behind? Do I dare to eat a peach?
       I shall wear white flannel trousers, and walk upon the beach.
       I have heard the mermaids singing, each to each.

c)   Anon comes Pyramus, sweet youth and tall,
           And finds his trusty Thisby's mantle slain;
       Whereat with blade, with bloody blameful blade,
           He bravely broach'd his boiling bloody breast;
       And Thisby, tarrying in the mulberry shade,
           His dagger drew, and died.

d)   I am not yet born, console me.
I fear that the human race may with tall walls wall me,
with strong drugs dope me, with wise lies lure me,
on black racks rack me, in blood-baths roll me.

e)   Oh, lift me as a wave, a leaf, a cloud!
I fall upon the thorns of life! I bleed!

f)   An Austrian army, awfully arrayed,
Boldly, by battery, besieged Belgrade;
Cossack commanders cannonading come —
Dealing destruction's devastating doom;
Every endeavour, engineers essay,
For fame, for fortune — fighting furious fray: —
Generals 'gainst generals grapple — gracious God!
How honours Heaven, heroic hardihood!

g)   And the dull wheel hums doleful through the day.

h)   And a jetty's jut, roped and ripe for hire,
The yellow boats lie yielding and lolling,
Jilted and jolted like jellies.

Having studied the quotations, can you say which of them (there
may possibly be more than one) contains alliteration that is:
i)   accidental: not intended as a poetic device by the poet;
ii)   regularly placed at the end of lines to create a balanced
musical effect;
iii)   written as a send-up of alliteration, ridiculing its excessive use
for melodramatic effects in the Elizabethan theatre;
iv)   to express a sense of monotony;
v)   to create stress on a particular sound, to suggest painful
feeling;
vi)   linked with internal rhyme and repetition to create a sense of
relentless uniformity;
vii)   a mere poetic trick; technique for its own sake;
viii)   deliberately concentrated and contrasted, suggesting unstable
movement.

2.   In the poem below, Ruth Pitter is reflecting on her own death.
She uses alliteration to create a musical effect, with soft sounds
for summer and sharper sounds for winter.

Call Not To Me

Call not to me when summer shines,
Death, for in summer I will not go;
When the tall grass falls in whispering lines

Call not loud from the shades below;
While under the willow the waters flow,
While willow waxes and waters wane,
When wind is slumbrous and water slow,
And woodbine waves in the wandering lane,
Call me not, for you call in vain,
Vain in the time when flowers blow.

But I will hear you when all is bare;
Call and welcome when leaves lie low;
When the dry bents hiss in the raving air
And shepherds from eastward smell the snow;
When the mead is left for the wind to mow,
And the storm is woodman to all the sere,
When hail is the seed the heavens sow,
When all is deadly and naught is dear —
Call and welcome, for I shall hear,
I shall be ready to rise and go.

Ruth Pitter

a) Trace the alliteration on 'l' and 'w' in the first verse.
b) Is there a minor alliterative pattern in the first verse also?
c) Is the alliteration carried over from the first verse to the second?
d) On what sound is the main alliteration in the second verse? Has the choice of sound any significance?
e) Give the meaning of line 6 and line 16.
f) On what personification is the poem based?
g) Give your reasons for supporting one of the following comments on the poem:

   i)   the alliteration adds to the effectiveness;
   ii) the alliteration is self-conscious and excessive.

3. *Inversnaid*

This darksome burn, horseback brown,
His rollrock highroad roaring down,
In coop and in comb the fleece of his foam
Flutes and low to the lake falls home.

A windpuff-bonnet of fawn-froth
Turns and twindles over the broth
Of a pool so pitchblack, fell-frowning,
It rounds and rounds Despair to drowning.

Degged with dew, dappled with dew
Are the groins of the braes that the brook treads through,
Wiry heathpacks, flitches of fern.
And the beadbonny ash that sits over the burn.

What would the world be, once bereft
Of wet and wildness? Let them be left,
O let them be left, wildness and wet;
Long live the weeds and the wilderness yet.

Gerard Manley Hopkins

The poem describes the progress of a vigorous stream (the 'burn')
through wild hilly country (the 'braes') to the lake below.
a) What themes of alliteration run through the poem?
b) Which lines contain perfectly balanced alliterative phrases?
c) How is alliteration reinforced in the final stanza?
d) What effect was Gerard Manley Hopkins aiming at when he
   devised the alliterative scheme of the poem?
e) How do you react to this poem? Criticise it, or write an
   appreciation of it; or do both.

ONOMATOPOEIA

Onomatopoeia — not a word that we come across very often in
English — and not all that easy to spell; but not really a difficult
word to understand. It describes a word that seems to imitate a
sound, like 'cuckoo'. Why is that particular bird named 'cuckoo' in
English? Obviously because the two sounds composing it imitate
the sound the bird makes. The word 'cuckoo', therefore, is
onomatopoeic.

Children are often taught onomatopoeic words when they first
learn to talk because they are easy to say and because they are
closely related in sound to the object that is being described: a dog
is a 'bow-wow', a gun is a 'bang-bang' and in the old days of steam
engines a train was a 'puff-puff'. In our everyday vocabulary we
use words that have a suggestion of onomatopoeia about them
because their sounds are linked with their meaning: words like
hiss, buzz, murmur, whisper, giggle, boom, atishoo, tinkle, wheeze,
swish, doom, crack, pop — and hundreds more.

When it comes to poetry the poet may use these and other
words as anyone else would use them, simply because they are the
most suitable to convey what he wants to say; and when he uses
'splash' and 'cuckoo' he is not really using onomatopoeia as a
special effect. He might, however, select a word with obvious care
for its onomatopoeic quality, as Ted Hughes does in:

> The tomcat still
> Grallochs odd dogs on the quiet

We may not know what 'grallochs' means, but it certainly sounds
like the way a tomcat might behave to an odd dog.

An onomatopoeic effect can be obtained from alliteration,
also, when the succession of similar or identical sounds underpins
the meaning. The most often quoted example of this in English
poetry is the two lines from Tennyson describing the sound of
doves and bees:

> The moan of doves in immemorial elms
> And the murmuring of innumerable bees

Look at the 'm' sounds in these lines. Are they there accidentally,
or has the poet chosen words with 'm' sounds in them because,
taken together, they suggest the cooing of doves and the humming
of bees?

51

Take another example of alliterative onomatopoeia: the description by Wordsworth of skating on a frozen lake:

All shod with steel
We hissed along the polished ice in games

The most prominent sounds in the lines are the 's' and 'sh' sounds which occur in shod, steel, hissed, polished, ice, games. You can see that these sounds correspond to some extent to the sound a skate might make when scraping over hard ice. The onomatopoeia, therefore, reinforces the meaning by linking it with appropriate sounds in the words.

Onomatopoeic rhythm can also be found in poetry. This occurs when the rhythm of the verse corresponds to the movement that is being described, such as the galloping of a horse, the marching of soldiers, the flow of a river, the movement of a train or, as in this example, the monotonous regularity and precision of a machine, from *The Secret of the Machines*, by Rudyard Kipling:

We can pull and haul and push and lift and drive,
We can print and plough and weave and heat and light,
We can run and race and swim and fly and dive,
We can see and hear and count and read and write!

1.   Below are some further examples of onomatopoeia in words, alliterative sounds and in rhythms. Study each one, then say what onomatopoeic effect the poet was aiming at and explain how he has achieved it.

a)   The cleanly rush of the mountain air
And the mumbling, grumbling humble bees.

b)   A host of screeching, scolding, scrabbling
sea-birds on the shore.

c)   What passing bell for these who die as cattle?
Only the monstrous anger of the guns.
Only the stuttering rifles' rapid rattle
Can patter out their hasty orisons.

d)   At home, suddenly I love you
As I hear the sharp clean trot of a pony down the road,
Succeeding sharp little sounds dropping into silence
Clear upon the long-drawn hoarseness of a train across the
valley.

e) . . . the taut tympan of the tom-toms rattling
In cracking fusillades, then dully grumbling
Like sullen thunder in far hills, then rumbling
Like earthquake underfoot, then sharply shattering
The zenith with a cataract of clattering
That peters to a pattering stuttering mutter

f) The beat of the rain
on the street is repeated
in afternoon feet
that emerge and recede
at the verge of the wet,
on teetering toes
and slithering shoes,
and shuffle to shelter
in doorway and lane.

g) Up the high hill he heaves a huge round stone;
The huge round stone, resulting with a bound,
Thunders impetuous down, and smokes along the ground.

2. *Jazz Fantasia*

Drum on your drums, batter on your banjoes,
sob on the long cool winding saxophones.
Go to it, O jazzmen.

Sling your knuckles on the bottoms of the happy
tin pans, let your trombones ooze, and go husha-
husha-hush with the slippery sand-paper.

Moan like an autumn wind high in the lonesome treetops,
        moan soft like
you wanted somebody terrible, cry like a racing car slipping
        away from a
motorcycle cop, bang-bang! you jazzmen, bang altogether
        drums, traps,
banjoes, horns, tin cans — make two people fight on the top
        of a stairway
and scratch each other's eyes in a clinch tumbling down the
        stairs.

Can the rough stuff . . . now a Mississippi steamboat pushes
        up the night
river with a hoo-hoo-hoo-oo . . . and the green lanterns
        calling to the high

soft stars . . . a red moon rides on the humps of the low
    river hills . . .
go to it, O jazzmen.

Carl Sandburg

a) Which three words suggest the sound made by the
    saxophones?
b) Can you explain what effect the poet is trying to create in the
    line beginning: *Sling your knuckles . . . ?*
c) What exactly is the instrumentalist doing who is going
    hush-a-hush-a-hush on the slippery sandpaper?
d) Which other word in line 7 repeats the sound of the word
    moan?
e) What is being described in the words: *hoo-hoo-oo?*
f) What other examples of onomatopoeia are there in the poem?
g) Can you explain why the poet says:
    *Make two people fight on the top of a stairway and scratch
        each other's eyes in a clinch tumbling down the stairs,*
h) Describe and comment on the diction of the poem.

3.   *Boots*
    (Infantry Columns)

We're foot-slog-slog-slog-sloggin' over Africa —
Foot-foot-foot-foot-sloggin' over Africa —
(Boots-boots-boots-boots-movin' up and down again!)
    There's no discharge in the war!

Seven-six-eleven-five-nine-an'-twenty mile to-day —
Four-eleven-seventeen-thirty-two the day before —
(Boots-boots-boots-boots-movin' up and down again!)
    There's no discharge in the war!

Don't-don't-don't-don't-look at what's in front of you.
(Boots-boots-boots-boots-movin' up an' down again);
Men-men-men-men-men go mad with watchin' 'em,
    An' there's no discharge in the war!

Try-try-try-try-to think o' something different —
Oh-my-God-keep-me from goin' lunatic!
(Boots-boots-boots-boots-movin' up an' down again!)
    There's no discharge in the war!

Count-count-count-count-the bullets in the bandoliers.
If-your-eyes-drop-they will get atop o' you!
(Boots-boots-boots-boots-movin' up and down again)
    There's no discharge in the war!

We-can-stick-out-'unger, thirst, an' weariness,
But-not-not-not-not the chronic sight of 'em —
(Boots-boots-boots-boots-movin' up an' down again,)
   An' there's no discharge in the war!

'Tain't-so-bad-by-day because o' company,
But night-brings-long-strings-o' forty thousand million
(Boots-boots-boots-boots-movin' up an' down again.)
   There's no discharge in the war!

I-'ave-marched-six-weeks in 'Ell an' certify
It-is-not-fire-devils, dark, or anything,
But boots-boots-boots-boots-movin' up an' down again,
   An' there's no discharge in the war!

Rudyard Kipling

a) The onomatopoeia is based on the strict regularity of the
rhythm, which, in turn, is based on the metre and the metrical
feet that compose it. Describe the metre and say what metrical
feet are used in the first three lines of each stanza.

b) Why is the rhythm changed in the fourth line?

c) How does the style of language (or diction) suggest the
character of the speaker?

d) What reasons are there for classing this poem as i) serious;
ii) humorous?

4. Read *Discord in Childhood* by D H Lawrence (page 111) and
answer the questions on the poem.

BALLADS

Have you ever picked up the words of a popular song just by hearing them over and over again? If you have, then you know something about the way the first ballads were passed on from one person to another and became part of popular and traditional poetry. A ballad is a short dramatic story told in verse and originally sung by a minstrel. The modern pop singer with his guitar and his lyric is a descendant of the original ballad singers of the fifteenth century, when an audience liked to listen to dramatic tales of love and heroism, of battles and crimes, of witches, ghosts and supernatural events — all told in simple verses without unnecessary literary trimmings, in a bold, direct vocabulary with the characters often breaking into the narrative and speaking for themselves. The story usually reached a tragic climax (for disaster and death were more popular than happy endings), but singer or narrator would not draw any moral; the listener could form his own conclusion, or simply feel satisfied that he had been well entertained.

Many of the best ballads were created in the fifteenth and sixteenth centuries and tell of the conflicts between the Scots and the English in the border country, for the ballad thrives on dramatic situations such as battles and communal strife. Also composed at this time were the many ballads about Robin Hood which expressed a popular feeling of rebelliousness towards feudalism and which idealised the hero-outlaw. Meanwhile, in less primitive surroundings, the ballad began to thrive as an expression of urban life and we got 'broadsides' — poems printed on small sheets which sold at fairs and market places for a penny each. These 'broadside ballads' were the ordinary person's main contact with the literary word and they were a source of news as well as of entertainment. They lasted even into the twentieth century and were finally superseded by the cheap, popular newspaper.

Emigration caused the spread of ballads from one country to another. Many of the traditional American ballads, for instance, have their origin in European countries, having been taken to the New World by immigrants. Wherever there were pioneering ventures and the exploration of new territories, ballads would be composed to dramatise the conflicts of the new life. Thus, we have the ballads of the American West, of the Yukon, of the sailors and the lumberjacks, of the plantation workers and of the swagmen of the Australian bush — ballads which were probably the only form of entertainment available to stave off the boredom of a lonely life in the outback, on the prairie or at sea. These are the 'genuine' folk ballads and songs, arising out of real situations, composed by non-literary people, shaped and altered as they became part of the oral tradition and eventually written down, published and 'fixed'.

During this time, of course, poets were composing 'literary' ballads, more refined in language and more subtly constructed than the ballads of the broadsides and of oral tradition. Some of them retold the old ballads, but all attempted to reproduce the characteristics of the genuine ballad; to write in four-line stanzas (quatrains), to use simple language, to move the story along rapidly and dramatically, and to create characters boldly rather than with psychological depth.

The ballad, like all literary forms, has undergone many changes over the centuries, but the basic intention of telling a story has remained and many contemporary poets and song-writers are continuing this literary tradition.

1. *Edward, Edward* is one of the earliest ballads and shows many of the characteristics of the traditional form — a dramatic story swiftly developed in bold, simple language:

'Why does your brand so drop with blood,
    Edward, Edward?
Why does your brand so drop with blood,
    And why so sad go ye, O?'

'O I have killed my hawk so good,
    Mother, mother;
O I have killed my hawk so good,
    And I had no more but he, O.'

'Your hawk's blood was never so red,
    Edward, Edward;
Your hawk's blood was never so red,
    My dear son, I tell thee, O.'

'O I have killed my red-roan steed,
    Mother, mother;
O I have killed my red-roan steed,
    That once was so fair and free, O.'

'Your steed was old, and you have got more,
    Edward, Edward;
Your steed was old, and you have got more,
    Some other dole ye dree, O.'

'O I have killed my father dear,
    Mother, mother;
O I have killed my father dear,
    Alas, and woe is me, O.'

'And what penance will ye dree for that,
    Edward, Edward?
What penance will ye dree for that,
    My dear son, now tell me O.'

'I'll set my foot in yonder boat,
    Mother, mother,
I'll set my foot in yonder boat,
    And I'll fare o'er the sea, O.'

'And what will ye do with your towers and your hall,
    Edward, Edward?
And what will ye do with your towers and your hall,
    That were so fair to see, O?'

'I'll let them stand till down they fall,
    Mother, mother;
I'll let them stand till down they fall,
    For here never more must I be, O.'

'And what will ye leave to your bairns and your wife,
    Edward, Edward?
And what will ye leave to your bairns and your wife,
    When ye go o'er the sea, O?'

'The world's room, let them beg through life,
    Mother, mother,
The world's room, let them beg through life,
    For them never more will I see, O.'

'And what will ye leave to your own mother dear,
    Edward, Edward?
And what will ye leave to your own mother dear,
    My dear son, now tell me, O?'

'The curse of hell from me shall ye bear,
    Mother, mother;
The curse of hell from me shall ye bear,
    Such counsels ye gave to me, O!'

Note: dree = endure, suffer.

a) Show how the story moves a step forward with each stanza by quoting a key line from each stanza.

b) Which stanza represents the first climax in the poem?

c) In which stanza does the poem reach its full climax? What is revealed? How does it throw new light on what has gone before?

d) The composer of the ballad has offered no comment on Edward or his mother, but allows them to reveal themselves through what they say. Give a brief sketch of both Edward and his mother and show how each of them reacted to the murder.

e) What relationship between Edward and his mother is implied in the poem?

f) Can you suggest what the situation might have been before the murder was committed?

g) Study the language of the ballad. Is it imaginative and figurative, or literal and direct? Give examples.

h) Describe the metrical structure and verse form. Considering the purpose of the ballad, what advantages do you think they would have?

i) Comment on the rhyme.

j) What use is made of repetition in the ballad? What reason might there be for it?

k) Why, when the ballad was first presented, would it benefit from a singer who was also a good actor?

l) Sum up your impression of the ballad, pointing out what you find effective or unsatisfactory about it. Remember, however, that it has its origins in the oral tradition and was composed for a society far different from ours.

2. *Young Hunting*

Light you down, light you down, love Henry, she said,
    And stay all night with me;
For I have a bed and a fireside too,
    And a candle burning bright.

I can't get down, nor I won't get down
    And stay all night with thee,
For that little girl in the old Declarn
    Would think so hard of me.

I will get down and I can get down
    And stay all night with thee,
For there's no little girl in the old Declarn
    That I love any better than thee.

But he slided down from his saddle skirts
    For to kiss her snowy white cheek,
She had a sharp knife in her hand,
    And she plunged it in him deep.

Must I ride to the East, must I ride to the West,
    Or anywhere under the sun,
To get some good and clever doctor
    For to cure this wounded man?

Neither ride to the East, neither ride to the West,
    Nor nowhere under the sun,
For there's no man but God's own hand
    Can cure this wounded man.

She took him by the long, yellow locks
    And also round the feet;
She plunged him into that doleful well,
    Some sixty fathoms deep.

And as she turned round to go home,
    She heard some pretty bird sing:
Go home, go home, you cruel girl,
    Lament and mourn for him.

Fly down, fly down, pretty parrot, she said,
    Fly down and go home with me.
Your cage shall be decked with beads of gold
    And hung in the willow tree.

I won't fly down, nor I can't fly down,
    And I won't go home with thee,
For you have murdered your own true love,
    And you might murder me.

I wish I had my little bow-ben
    And had it with a string;
I'd surely shoot that cruel bird
    That sits on the briers and sings.

I wish you had your little bow-ben
    And had it with a string;
I'd surely fly from vine to vine;
    You could always hear me sing.

This is a twentieth-century version of a ballad known in
eighteenth-century Scotland, with perhaps earlier Danish parallels.

a) What do you think the situation was before the events in the ballad take place?

b) Henry is speaking in the second and third stanzas. What sudden change of mind seems to occur between these two stanzas?

c) Do you think a similar change of mind — or of feeling — on the part of the girl has occurred between stanzas four and five?

d) In what way are these features characteristic of the traditional ballad?

e) The characters in the old ballads are usually depicted boldly, without great psychological depth. Would you say this is true of the character of the girl in the poem? Describe her character and say what subtlety you think there is in the way it is presented.

f) The parrot is an unexpected element in the poem. It is obviously unrealistic and must be interpreted in a special way. What evidence is there for interpreting it as a symbol of the girl's conscience — the nagging sense of guilt at murdering her lover that will not go away? What other possibilities are there for understanding the role of the parrot in the poem?

g) In what way are the verse form and the rhyme characteristic of the ballad?

h) When a phrase or a line is repeated in a ballad with some slight change in the wording it is called *incremental repetition*. What examples can you find in the poem? Why do you think that incremental repetition was such a common feature of the old ballads?

i) Compare the use made of conversation and description in the ballad. Why should one predominate over the other?

j) Give your impression of the ballad as a whole, saying what you found of interest — or what you found lacking — in the story, the characterisation and the poetic technique.

3. Modern versions of the old ballads are becoming increasingly popular. What examples are there in contemporary music? Arrange a session of listening to some examples and discuss whether or not they are improved with their new treatment. What can account for the revival of this form of poetry?

BLANK VERSE

Henry Howard, Earl of Surrey, though he did not live to see the
publication of his poems (he was executed at the age of thirty by
Henry VIII), was responsible for introducing blank verse into
England through his translation of books II and IV of Virgil's
Aeneid. It was called 'blank' because it was unrhymed, but it was
'verse' because it conformed to a strict metrical pattern: ten
syllables and five stresses to a line; and as the stresses were based
on iambic feet, the line was called an iambic pentameter — perhaps
the most widely used metrical shape in English poetry. It became
the medium of most of the verse drama in Elizabethan and later
periods, it dominated narrative poetry in later centuries and it is
still being used by poets today.

   To write verse drama that observes the rule of five stresses to a
line, each stress based on an iambic foot, might seem to be
over-restrictive and to hamper a dramatist's expression rather than
aid it; and this certainly did happen in the early blank verse plays
when there was a pause at the end of every line and the metre was
thumped out with monotonous regularity; but blank verse,
particularly in the hands of a master such as Shakespeare, matured
rapidly and though the basic pattern remained, there were
variations introduced which made the verse much more flexible
and natural in its expression. The following speech, from *King
Lear*, shows how close the rhythms are to natural speech whilst
still conforming the pentameter:

> You see me here, you gods, a poor old man,
> As full of grief as age; wretched in both!
> If it be you that stir these daughters' hearts
> Against their father, fool me not so much
> To bear it tamely; touch me with noble anger,
> And let not women's weapons, water-drops,
> Stain my man's cheeks! No, you unnatural hags,
> I will have such revenges on you both
> That all the world shall — I will do such things —
> What they are yet I know not, — but they shall be
> The terrors of the earth. You think I'll weep;
> No, I'll not weep:
> I have full cause of weeping, but this heart
> Shall break into a hundred thousand flaws
> Or ere I'll weep. O fool! I shall go mad.

One departure from strict regularity comes in the use of *enjambment*, or run-on lines, and in the pauses occurring in the middle of the line *(caesuras)* instead of at the end. Another is in the variation in the number of syllables: there are ten syllables to each line, except line 5, which contains twelve, line 10, which contains eleven, and line 12, which has only four. Then, if you count the stresses you will find it difficult to space them out evenly in each line. The first line is a perfect iambic pentameter:

Yoǔ sée mě hére, yǒu góds, ǎ póor oǐd mán

— but this perfect tick-tock rhythm is not kept up for long. Where does it begin to change? You will find that the stress-pattern that arises from natural speech soon takes over and the blank verse structure is hidden. Line 12 is a good example of Shakespeare's deliberately breaking the five-stress pattern, with the simplicity of:

No, I'll not weep:

There couldn't be five stresses in this line of four monosyllables. If you were an actor playing King Lear, how many words would you stress in this line: one, two, three or four? Whichever you chose, you could still make dramatic sense of the line. There is, therefore, the basic pattern of ten syllables and five stresses, but this is varied by the dramatist and it is further changed when the human voice gives the lines expression and meaning. The monotony that might have resulted from the blank verse, therefore — and which can be felt when the verse is badly spoken — is avoided and replaced by a strong natural rhythm.

Blank verse continued to be used in the centuries following the Elizabethan period and it reached a high point in the poetry of John Milton (1608-74), who used it for his epic poem *Paradise Lost* (twelve books, about 1,000 lines each). Milton, having rejected rhyme as 'troublesome' and nothing more than 'the jingling sound of like-endings', introduced a new strictness into blank verse and made it conform more rigidly to the rules than the Elizabethan dramatists had done. The suitability of blank verse for long narrative poems was proved by its being used in the nineteenth century by such poets as Wordsworth, Keats, Browning, Tennyson and Matthew Arnold, and in the twentieth century by Robert Frost and John Betjeman. But to many modern poets blank verse has a 'cosy' ring about it. It is perhaps too neat, too carefully balanced, too flat, to make an appeal to writers who are seeking freer and more original forms in which to express themselves. It has not, therefore, achieved the popularity it had a century ago; and with the plays of Shakespeare still holding their own on the English stage there is hardly likely to be a revival of blank verse in the modern theatre. What has been called 'the distinctive poetic form of our language' seems for the moment, therefore, to be in partial eclipse.

1. The first example of blank verse for closer study is another passage from *Sohrab and Rustum.* Sohrab, the young representative of the Tartars, engages in a duel with Rustum, the old, renowned Persian champion. It is not until Rustum calls out his own name, however, that Sohrab realises he is in combat with his own father. Shocked by the knowledge, he drops his defence and is fatally wounded. Rustum, who did not know he was fighting his son, learns whom he has slain.

> But in the gloom they fought, with bloodshot eyes
> And labouring breath; first Rustum struck the shield
> Which Sohrab held stiff out: the steel-spik'd spear
> Rent the tough plates, but failed to reach the skin,
> And Rustum pluck'd it back with angry groan.
> Then Sohrab with his sword smote Rustum's helm,
> Nor clove its steel quite through: but all the crest
> He shore away, and that proud horsehair plume,
> Never till now defiled, sunk to the dust;
> And Rustum bow'd his head; but the gloom
> Grew blacker: thunder rumbled in the air,
> And lightnings rent the cloud; and Ruksh, the horse,
> Who stood at hand, utter'd a dreadful cry:
> No horse's cry was that, most like the roar
> Of some pain'd desert lion, who all day
> Has trail'd the hunter's javelin in his side,
> And comes at night to die upon the sand:—
> The two hosts heard that cry, and quak'd for fear,
> And Oxus curdled as it cross'd his stream.
> But Sohrab heard, and quail'd not, but rush'd on,
> And struck again; and again Rustum bow'd
> His head; but this time all the blade, like glass,
> Sprang in a thousand shivers on the helm,
> And in his hand the hilt remain'd alone.
> Then Rustum rais'd his head: his dreadful eyes
> Glar'd, and he shook on high his menacing spear,
> And shouted, Rustum! Sohrab heard that shout,
> And shrank amaz'd: back he recoil'd one step,
> And scann'd with blinking eyes the advancing form:
> And then he stood bewilder'd; and he dropp'd
> His covering shield, and the spear pierc'd his side.

He reel'd, and staggering back, sunk to the ground.
And then the gloom dispers'd, and the wind fell,
And the bright sun broke forth, and melted all
The cloud; and the two armies saw the pair;
Saw Rustum standing, safe upon his feet,
And Sohrab, wounded, on the bloody sand.

a) Analyse i) the regularity and ii) the variations in the blank
verse.
b) Show the dramatic development of the narrative by describing
the blows that are struck and the effects they had.
c) Show how the 'unnaturalness' of the fight between father and
son is suggested symbolically by: i) the weather; ii) Ruksh;
iii) the River Oxus.
d) Describe, with examples, the style of language used in the
poem.

2. The second example of blank verse is from *Paradise Lost*, by
John Milton (1608-74). Satan has rebelled against God, been
defeated, and been banished from heaven. He and his followers
have just entered hell. Satan speaks:

"Is this the region, this the soil, the clime,"
Said then the lost Archangel, "this the seat
That we must change for heaven? — this mournful gloom
For that celestial light? Be it so, since he
Who now is sovereign can dispose and bid
What shall be right: farthest from him is best,
Whom reason hath equalled, force hath made supreme
Above his equals. Farewell, happy fields,
Where joy for ever dwells! Hail, horrors! hail,
Infernal World! and thou, profoundest hell,
Receive thy new possessor — one who brings
A mind not to be changed by place or time.
The mind is its own place, and in itself
Can make a heaven of hell, a hell of heaven.
What matter where, if I be still the same,
And what I should be, all, but less than he
Whom thunder hath made greater? Here at least
We shall be free; the Almighty hath not built
Here for his envy, will not drive us hence:
Here we may reign secure; and, in my choice,
To reign is worth ambition, though in hell:
Better to reign in hell than serve in heaven.

a) Show, by giving examples, how flexible the blank verse is.

b) What two phrases from the beginning of the speech show the contrast between heaven and hell?

c) In line 7 Satan says that he and God are equals in reason. What, then, according to Satan, has made God supreme?

d) Where does Satan return to the idea of God's power later in the speech?

e) Where in the speech is it apparent that Satan recognises heaven as a happier place than hell?

f) Express in your own way:
   The mind is its own place, and in itself
   Can make a heaven of hell, a hell of heaven.

g) The above quotation is an aphorism — a short, pithy statement that seems to express a truth. Quote another of Satan's aphorisms.

h) What consolations does Satan find in having to live in hell?

i) Express your own reaction to Milton's portrayal of Satan.

HEROIC COUPLETS

When one of the Broker's Men in *Cinderella* declares:

> My lord, my mate and me is quite dumbfounded
> By this 'ere theory you've just propounded —
> But coronets, as you so rightly say,
> Is worth more than kind 'arts any day.

he is using a rather run-down version of one of the great English
poetic forms: herioc couplets. A 'couplet' means a couple of
rhymed lines: 'heroic' means that each line consists of ten syllables
with five stresses — blank verse, in fact, except that the lines
rhyme in pairs instead of remaining 'blank'. These couplets
occurred occasionally in medieval verse, but it was Chaucer who
first developed them into a recognisable poetic form. He
composed some 16,000 lines of them. They were popular with
Elizabethan poets and with dramatists, who found the rhyme a
useful way of indicating the end of a scene in a play, and they
were used for plays with heroic themes in the seventeenth century
— great epic dramas with titles like *The Siege of Rhodes*, *The
Indian Emperor* and *The Conquest of Granada*. The rhymed
couplets gave the plays an eloquent and grandiose effect, but they
also made the speeches seem contrived and unnatural and the style
was eventually dropped, to be revived in the bouncing banalities of
pantomime rhyme.

Heroic couplets reached their peak of perfection during the
seventeenth and eighteenth centuries in the satirical poetry of
John Dryden and Alexander Pope. The couplet seemed to
discipline the poet into condensing his meaning into sharp,
balanced phrases with the rhyme adding a final clinching flourish:

> Words are like leaves: and where they most abound
> Much fruit of sense beneath is rarely found

> The hungry judges soon the sentence sign,
> And wretches hang that jurymen may dine.

Pope's satirical portrait of Addison, a contemporary writer and
politician with whom Pope had quarrelled, shows the skill with
which the couplet can be used. The lines contain evenly balanced
phrases, one often contrasting with the other, and each couplet is
a separate, compressed comment on Addison's character. It is a
powerful and incisive portrait, combining scorn and insinuation,

67

yet brilliantly subtle and delicate in its use of language. Addison,
Pope says, would:

> Damn with faint praise, assent with civil leer,
> And, without sneering, teach the rest to sneer;
> Willing to wound, and yet afraid to strike,
> Just hint a fault, and hesitate dislike;
> Alike reserved to blame, or to commend,
> A timorous foe, and a suspicious friend;
> Dreading e'en fools, by flatterers besieged,
> And so obliging, that he ne'er obliged;
> Like Cato, give his little senate laws,
> And sit attentive to his own applause;

In addition to satirical verse, heroic couplets were successfully
used for narrative verse, particularly in the eighteenth and
nineteenth centuries. George Crabbe (1754-1832) demonstrated
the flexibility of the form in his long narrative poem, *Peter
Grimes*. Though sticking strictly to the pentameter and seldom
deviating from full rhyme, Crabbe got a great deal of variety into
his poem, which is rich in descriptive passages, dramatic incident
and portrayal of character. Peter Grimes is a young fisherman who
drinks and gambles and does a little stealing on the side. He lives
alone in a hovel and is bored with life. He decides that he should
have someone to work for him, preferably a young boy whom he
can bully and beat. He applies to a London workhouse and for a
small sum acquires a young apprentice:

> Peter had heard there were in London then, —
> Still have they being! — workhouse-clearing men,
> Who, undisturb'd by feelings just or kind,
> Would parish-boys to needy tradesmen bind:
> They in their want a trifling sum would take,
> And toiling slaves of piteous orphans make.
> Such Peter sought, and when a lad was found,
> The sum was dealt him, and the slave was bound.
> Some few in town observed in Peter's trap
> A boy, with jacket blue and woollen cap:
> But none inquired how Peter used the rope,
> Or what the bruise that made the stripling stoop;
> None could the ridges on his back behold,
> None sought him shiv'ring in the winter's cold;
> None put the question, — 'Peter dost thou give,
> The boy his food? — What, man! the lad must live.
> Consider, Peter, let the child have bread,
> He'll serve thee better if he's stroked and fed.'

None reason'd thus and some, on hearing cries,
Said calmly, 'Grimes is at his exercise.'
Pinn'd, beaten, cold, pinch'd, threaten'd, and abused —
His efforts punished and his food refused, —
Awake tormented, — soon aroused from sleep, —
Struck if he wept, and yet compell'd to weep,
The trembling boy dropp'd down and strove to pray,
Received a blow, and trembling turn'd away
Or sobb'd and hid his piteous face; — while he,
The savage master, grinn'd in horrid glee:
He'd now the power he ever loved to show,
A feeling being subject to his blow.
Thus lived the lad, in hunger, peril, pain,
His tears despised, his supplications vain:
Compell'd by fear to lie, by need to steal,
His bed uneasy and unbless'd his meal,
For three sad years the boy his tortures bore,
And then his pains and trials were no more.
'How died he, Peter?' when the people said,
He growl'd — 'I found him lifeless in his bed;'
Then tried for softer tone, and sigh'd, 'Poor Sam is dead.'
Yet murmurs were there, and some questions ask'd —
How he was fed, how punish'd, and how task'd?
Much they suspected, but they little proved,
And Peter pass'd untroubled and unmoved.

a) Though the verse is very regular, every line containing ten
syllables and five stresses, with the rhyme almost faultless —
yet the poem doesn't seem stilted or contrived. How has
Crabbe introduced a naturalness of expression into his verse?

b) Which phrase in the following line provides an alliterative
balance to *a trifling sum* in line 5?

c) Line 21 stands out as being slightly irregular. Can you say in
what way it differs from the others? Why should Crabbe want
to draw attention to this line?

d) Do you think the line: *The savage master, grinn'd in horrid
glee* is an exaggeration (reminiscent, perhaps, of an evil
character in a melodrama) or an acceptable description of
Peter Grimes?

e) Can you find some couplets, each line of which falls neatly
into two balanced halves?

f) Which lines show the greatest compression of language?

g) Which couplet seems to sum up Peter's basic nature?

h) What criticism of the townspeople is implied in this passage?

i) Describe Peter's attitude towards the boy and attempt an explanation of it.

j) What do you think the townspeople suspected?

THE SONNET

Sonetto in Italian meant 'little sound or song' and 'sonnet' in English means a short poem of fourteen lines. It was introduced into England from Italy in the early sixteenth century by Sir Thomas Wyatt, who, besides being a poet of some distinction, was also a soldier, a diplomat and a survivor of the Tower. Wyatt travelled widely on the Continent, became acquainted with the sonnets of the Italian poet Petrarch and began writing sonnets himself. By the end of the century the sonnet had become a popular poetic form and several poets produced cycles or sequences of sonnets addressed to a particular person or linked to a theme. The most accomplished sonnet-sequence is Shakespeare's, published in 1609 and consisting of 154 numbered sonnets on the themes of love, time and change. Most of the sonnets were addressed to a young man whose identity remains unknown; others were written to 'the Dark Lady of the Sonnets', who remains equally enigmatic, though speculation as to who she was ranges from Queen Elizabeth to a negro abbess.

Although all sonnets contain fourteen lines and most of them are written in five-stress, ten-syllable lines, the rhyme schemes can differ widely. The Petrarchan sonnet, introduced by Wyatt, was based upon a rhyme scheme that divided the sonnet into an octave (the first eight lines) and a sestet (the remaining six lines):

abba abba cde cde or abba abba cd cd cd

The sestet could be varied, but there was never a rhymed couplet at the end.

The English sonnet, first developed by the Earl of Surrey and adopted by Shakespeare for his long sequence, consisted of three quatrains and a couplet, which permitted a slightly easier pattern of rhyme than the Petrarchan model did:

abab cdcd efef gg

The difference may not seem to be very significant, yet it had a marked influence upon the development of thought in the poem. The Petrarchan sonnet fell into two distinct parts: the statement of the problem in the octave and the answer to it in the sestet. There was, therefore, a turning point in the argument after the eighth line, a pivot on which the two parts of the sonnet balanced. The Shakespearean sonnet, as it came to be called, fell into three statements that were answered or resolved in the final couplet,

71

which had a clinching effect on the argument, often reversing the thought expressed in the preceding lines. This was typically Elizabethan and it gave the English sonnet a character quite distinct from the Italian one. The concluding couplet could be a witty and dramatic climax to the thought, or it could become a verbal gimmick which brought into question the sincerity of the poem. Milton's sonnets, however, eschewed the 'cleverness' which was typical of the Elizabethan sonnet and brought a new seriousness and intellectual passion to the form. He went back to the Petrarchan model of octave and sestet, often running the two together to produce a more powerful and unified statement.

These two dominant rhyme-schemes, with variations, were used by poets from the sixteenth century onwards and it was not until the twentieth century that major changes began to take place in the accepted form. The fourteen lines could be split up into separate verses, the five-stress decasyllabic line might be dropped, the rhyme-scheme was sometimes abandoned altogether — yet the fourteen lines remained as the sonnet's essential characteristic.

The form has remained popular because it can be used for such a variety of purposes. Starting off as a 'little song', usually of love, it has been used by poets for religious confession, political address, the description and evocation of nature, character portrayal, personal reflection, and even as a vehicle for telling a short story. Its great virtue is the compression of thought and expression that the fourteen lines demand and this discipline has produced some remarkable poetic miniatures.

1.   *The Vixen*

> Among the taller wood with ivy hung,
> The old fox plays and dances round her young.
> She snuffs and barks if any passes by
> And swings her tail and turns, prepared to fly.
> The horseman hurries by, she bolts to see,
> And turns again, from danger never free.
> If any stands she runs among the poles
> And barks and snaps and drives them in their holes.
> The shepherd sees them and the boy goes by
> And gets a stick and progs the hole to try.
> They get all still and lie in safety sure,
> And out again when everything's secure,
> And start and snap at blackbirds bouncing by,
> To fight and catch the great white butterfly.

John Clare

a) In what way is the form of the poem typical of the sonnet?
b) How does it differ from the standard sonnet forms?
c) What dangers threaten the foxes and how does the old fox react to them?
d) What contrast to these dangers is there in the lives of the foxes?
e) You probably won't find *progs* in your dictionary. Make an intelligent guess at the meaning.
f) John Clare was a countryman and had obviously watched foxes very closely. What details in the poem seem to you to be particularly well observed?
g) Study the language of the poem. In what sense would you call it 'poetic'?

2. *Still-Life*

Through the open French window the warm sun
lights up the polished breakfast-table, laid
round a bowl of crimson roses, for one —
a service of Worcester porcelain, arrayed
near it a melon, peaches, figs, small hot
rolls in a napkin, fairy rack of toast,
butter in ice, high silver coffee-pot,
and, heaped on a salver, the morning's post.

She comes over the lawn, the young heiress,
from her early walk in her garden-wood
feeling that life's a table set to bless
her delicate desires with all that's good,

that even the unopened future lies
like a love-letter, full of sweet surprise.

Elizabeth Daryush

a) Is the rhyme-scheme Petrarchan or Shakespearean?
b) To what extent does the division of the subject of the poem follow the divisions of the rhyme-scheme?
c) The metre of the traditional sonnet is based on a line of five stresses and ten syllables. Does this sonnet conform to the tradition?
d) How do you think the poet achieves the smooth flow of the verse?
e) What is the poet suggesting about the heiress's *unopened future* in the final couplet?
f) What does the phrase 'still-life' mean when applied to a painting? What significance has it as the title of the poem?

3.   *Who's Who*

The shilling life will give you all the facts:
How Father beat him, how he ran away,
What were the struggles of his youth, what acts
Made him the greatest figure of his day:
Of how he fought, fished, hunted, worked all night;
Though giddy, climbed new mountains; named a sea:
Some of the last researchers even write
Love made him weep his pints like you and me.
With all his honours on, he sighed for one
Who, say astonished critics, lived at home;
Did little jobs about the house with skill
And nothing else; could whistle; would sit still
Or potter round the garden; answered some
Of his long marvellous letters, but kept none.

W H Auden

The *shilling life* in the first line refers to the paperback edition (in those days costing one shilling) of the biography of the famous man who is the subject of the poem.

a)   Up to which point does the rhyme-scheme follow the Shakespearean pattern?
b)   How is the subject of the poem related to the octave and the sestet?
c)   Is the sonnet metrically regular?
d)   Give three examples of the 'greatness' of the man and three contrasting phrases showing the ordinariness of the woman.
e)   Which line in the first part of the sonnet makes the famous man seem much like anybody else?
f)   Why were the critics *astonished?*
g)   Which character does the poet appear to approve of: the man of fame or the woman who stayed at home?
h)   Why, in your opinion, did the woman keep none of the man's letters?
i)   Which word in the last line of the poem is not intended to be taken literally?
j)   The title of the poem has a special meaning. What is it? What bearing has it on the poem?

For further study of the sonnet, read: *The Tomb of David Hume* by Alan Bold (page 111), *After dark vapours have oppress'd our plains* by John Keats (page 112) and *To me, fair friend, you never can be old* by William Shakespeare (page 113).

FREE VERSE

If you were a poet and you decided to write a poem in stanza
form, using rhyme and regular metre, you wouldn't exactly be
writing spontaneously. Verse of that kind doesn't spring
ready-made from a writer's pen and in order to stick to your metre
and rhyme scheme you might have to diverge slightly from your
intended meaning, remembering, perhaps, as you did so, John
Wood's epitaph:

> Here lies John Bun,
> He was killed by a gun.
> His name was not Bun, but Wood,
> But Wood would not rhyme with gun, but Bun would.

You might find that the restrictions you were imposing upon your
poem were so limiting that you wanted to throw them off
altogether and write 'freely', without metrical restraint, saying
what you had to say as directly and honestly as possible. If you
did this you would be following the argument for writing 'free
verse' — verse free of all metrical constraints, yet still containing
the qualities that we recognise as belonging to poetry.

Though there had been unrhymed, loosely-structured verse
written in England for centuries, it wasn't until the nineteenth
century that free verse (or *vers libre*, as it was called in France,
where it originated) became recognised as a poetic movement. It
was used by the American poet, Walt Whitman, whose *Leaves of
Grass* (1855) is one of the landmarks in free verse, and established
itself as the characteristic poetic style of the twentieth century.

By now, most people agree that poetry doesn't need to rhyme
or to be set out in regular verses to be genuine poetry: there are
other characteristics by which we recognise poetry besides these.
What are these characteristics? How do we recognise, without the
usual indications, that a piece of writing is poetry, rather than
prose? There is, first, the visual sign: the arrangement of the
writing on the printed page tells us that we are looking at a form
of verse, rather than prose; but a more significant indication is the
sound of the writing when it is read aloud — particularly the
rhythm the sound creates. Free verse may have given up regular
metre, but it hasn't given up rhythm completely; it has simply
changed to a freer, less calculated rhythm — what has been called
'the spontaneous expression of inner rhythm' — and it is this that
partly distinguishes verse from prose. In addition to spontaneous

rhythm there is the language of poetry, which need not be any the less rich and imaginative because it is not in harness with rhyme and metre. Free verse is not, therefore, an 'easy option' in poetry; to write it well requires as much feeling for language and poetic technique as traditional verse does. 'No *vers* is *libre*,' T S Eliot has written, 'for the man who wants to do a good job.'

D H Lawrence was one of the great exponents of free verse during this century and a study of the opening of his poem *Mountain Lion* will show some of the qualities of this verse form.

Lawrence and a friend are walking up the Lobo Valley in Mexico when they see two Mexicans coming towards them:

> Climbing through the January snow, into the Lobo Canyon
> Dark grow the spruce-trees, blue is the balsam, water sounds
>   still unfrozen, and the trail is still evident.
>
> Men!
> Two men!
> Men! The only animal in the world to fear!
>
> They hesitate.
> We hesitate.
> They have a gun.
> We have no gun.
>
> Then we all advance, to meet.
>
> Two Mexicans, strangers, emerging out of the dark and snow
>   and inwardness of the Lobo Valley.
> What are they doing here on this vanishing trail?
>
> What is he carrying?
> Something yellow.
> A deer?
>
> *Qué tiene, amigo?*   [*What are you carrying, friend?*]
> *León* —
> He smiles, foolishly, as if he were caught doing wrong.
> And we smile, foolishly, as if we didn't know.
> He is quite gentle and dark-faced.
>
> It is a mountain lion,
> A long, long slim cat, yellow like a lioness.
> Dead.

At a glance, the poem has no form, it is not written in regular stanzas. The lines vary in length from one word to about nineteen. When we read the poem we discover an absence of rhyme and metre. However, the poem reads easily. The sentences seem to

flow naturally, without contrivance, without an obvious striving
after poetic effect. We can almost hear the author speaking, we
can share his thoughts; and the use of the present tense makes us
feel that the incident is happening now, at this minute. Is it
poetry? The answer to that will depend on what we expect from
poetry, but there are undoubtedly qualities here which we identify
as poetic. There is, for instance, rhythm. If we read the lines:

> Dark grow the spruce-trees, blue is the balsam, water sounds
>   still unfrozen, and the trail is still evident.

we shall find ourselves stressing dark, blue, water and trail — and
thus creating a rhythm based on the four phrases which these
words introduce. A new rhythm begins with:

> Men!
> Two men!
> Men!

Then, in the following section there is a neatly balanced rhythm
created by the repetitions:

> They hesitate.
> We hesitate.
> They have a gun.
> We have no gun.

A similar parallelism is used later in the poem with:

> He smiles, foolishly, . . .
> And we smile, foolishly, . . .

The short rhythmical sentences and exclamations are offset by the
longer flowing statements:

> Two Mexicans, strangers, emerging out of the dark and snow
>   and inwardness of the Lobo Valley.

There is thus a variety of rhythms created in this part of the poem,
quite different from the regular rhythms of metrical verse and the
flatter rhythms of prose.

Yet there is still more that can be seen as typical of poetry.
The phrase 'dark grow the spruce-trees' would normally be
written, 'the spruce-trees grow dark', but we are prepared to
accept the inversion because it helps to stress the important word
dark and gives the phrase a poetic impact. We note also the line:

> A long, long slim cat, yellow like a lioness

with its six 'l's', three in each half of the line, leading up to the
sudden anticlimax *Dead* in the following line. All this is part of the
language of poetry.

A further quality Lawrence brings to this poem, which arises directly out of its being free verse, is the dramatic sense. The reader feels he is there, walking up the canyon, because the language and the form of the poem convey this sense of immediacy. The tension in the poem builds up when the two Mexicans appear and the author remarks:

Men! The only animal in the world to fear!

We learn that the two Mexicans have a gun; Lawrence and his companion have no gun. The implication is obvious, but the tension lessens as the four men meet. Then another question arises: what are the men doing on this vanished trail, and what are they carrying? The answer — after a wrong guess — is that they have been hunting and they are carrying a mountain lion which they have shot. The poem and the situation become more relaxed. The Mexican is not dangerous — quite the opposite: gentle and rather embarrassed at being caught carrying the mountain lion. The poem has moved from a dark, possibly dangerous situation, through a puzzling question and on to a dramatic answer. The free verse has permitted Lawrence to write in a relaxed, apparently spontaneous style and his changing thoughts and reactions are given an immediacy that would have been difficult to create in another poetic form.

1. Read the continuation of *Mountain Lion* and answer the questions that follow it.

He trapped her this morning, he says, smiling foolishly.

Lift up her face,
Her round, bright face, bright as frost.
Her round, fine-fashioned head, with two dead ears;
And stripes in the brilliant frost of her face, sharp, fine dark
    rays,
Dark, keen, fine rays in the brilliant frost of her face.
Beautiful dead eyes.

Hermoso es!   [*It is beautiful!*]

They go out towards the open;
We go on into the gloom of Lobo.

And above the trees I found her lair,
A hole in the blood-orange brilliant rocks that stick up, a
    little cave.
And bones, and twigs, and a perilous ascent.

So, she will never leap up that way again, with the yellow
    flash of a mountain lion's long shoot!

And her bright striped frost-face will never watch any more,
    out of the shadow of the cave in the blood-orange rock,
Above the trees of the Lobo dark valley-mouth!

Instead, I look out.

And out to the dim of the desert, like a dream, never real;
To the snow of the Sangre de Cristo mountains, the ice of the
    mountains of Picoris,
And near across at the opposite steep of snow, green trees
    motionless standing in snow, like a Christmas toy.

And I think in this empty world there was room for me and a
    mountain lion.
And I think in the world beyond, how easily we might spare
    a million or two of humans
And never miss them.
Yet what a gap in the world, the missing white frost-face of
    that slim yellow mountain lion!

a) Read again the description of the mountain lion's face,
   beginning *Lift up her face.* How does Lawrence make use of
   repetition to create a series of rhythms in these lines?
b) Is repetition used elsewhere in the poem?
c) Would you say that the poem is written in a conversational
   style of language or not? Give some examples.
d) You would probably agree that the poem has a strong visual
   content: it is easy to imagine the canyon, the snow mountains
   and the mountain lion from Lawrence's descriptions. Trace the
   references to colour in the complete poem; then show how the
   background has been depicted in contrast to the colour.
e) What do you think Lawrence chiefly regrets about the killing
   of the mountain lion?
f) The following lines from the poem have often caused some
   controversy:

   *And I think in the world beyond, how easily we might spare
       a million or two of humans
   And never miss them.*

What do you think of these lines? Are we to take them
literally and assume that Lawrence means what he says — that
he is indifferent to the fate of millions of human beings? Or is
there some other way of interpreting them which would allow
us to think that Lawrence was not completely inhuman?

2. For other examples of poems written in free verse, study:
    The Hill (page 114) and *Visiting Hour* (page 115)

LIMERICKS

The limerick is the only form of poem that no-one seems to have a resistance to — probably because it is short (not many poeple like 'long' poems), it is easily understood and it is usually funny.

It origins are something of a mystery. One theory has it that it was brought to Limerick in Ireland in 1700 by returning veterans of the French war; another that it originated in nursery rhymes published in *Mother Goose Melodies for Children* in 1719. The form was certainly known to John 'The Gay' O'Tuomy, landlord of a tavern in Limerick, who wrote in the mid-eighteenth century:

> I sell the best brandy and sherry,
> To make my good customers merry,
>   But at times their finances
>   Run short, as it chances,
> And then I feel very sad, very.

The limerick crossed the Irish Sea and first appeared in published form in *The History of Sixteen Wonderful Old Women* in 1821 and in *Anecdotes and Adventures of Fifteen Gentlemen* in 1822. It was this latter volume which caught the interest of Edward Lear, who was later to set the limerick on the road to universal popularity. Lear was an artist who had been engaged by the Earl of Derby at his country mansion to make coloured paintings of the Earl's collection of parrots. The Earl had a number of grand-children whom Lear amused by writing 'limericks' (a word never used by Lear himself), which he illustrated with amusing little sketches. He published his collection in 1846 in *The Book of Nonsense* — and the limerick never looked back.

Because the limerick had an easily recognisable form — five lines, rhyming a a b b a, with three stresses in the first, second and fifth lines and two stresses in the third and fourth — and because the subject was always an eccentric character identified with a certain place, it proved comparatively easy for amateurs to imitate and it inspired numerous competitions in magazines. In 1907 two London magazines ran limerick competitions and had thousands of entries — at sixpence a time. The sale of sixpenny postal orders shot up from one hundred thousand to over a quarter of a million in a month. Since then, limerick competitions have been organised by radio and television programmes and have attracted a vast number of entries.

The style of the limerick has changed slightly in the century or more since the publication of *The Book of Nonsense*. Lear's limericks usually end with a line that is almost a repeat of the first line and to the modern ear this seems to fall a little flat. Today, a more witty last line is preferred, something that gives a comic twist or climax to the preceding lines. Limericks have also left behind the gentle dottiness they had in Victorian times to become more bawdy and irreverent. Perhaps this accounts for their continued popularity: they form a respectable outlet for a healthy vulgarity.

1. Below is a selection of limericks from all periods, some of them anonymous. They demonstrate the continuity of the limerick in English writing, but also show that it is more varied in its content than is often supposed. Is it always a nonsensical verse? Can it contain, for instance, a serious idea, a real understanding of character, a moral, or a social criticism? Read the limericks, then decide:
a)   which are 'good' limericks, and why they are good;
b)   which contain, in humorous disguise, an idea that makes sense;
c)   which show a delight in tricks of language;
d)   which contain an insight into human nature.

There was an old man who said: 'How
Shall I flee from this terrible cow?
　　　I will sit on this style,
　　　And continue to smile,
Which may soften the heart of that Cow.

Edward Lear

There was a young man of Montrose
Who had pockets in none of his clothes.
　　　When asked by his lass
　　　Where he carried his brass,
He said, 'Darling, I pay through the nose.'

Arnold Bennett

There was a young man of St Bees,
Who was stung on the nose by a wasp.
　　　When they said, 'Does it hurt?'
　　　He replied, 'Not at all,
I'm glad it wasn't a hornet!'

There was a young man who said, 'Damn!
It is borne in upon me I am
  An engine that moves
  In predestinate grooves,
I'm not even a bus — I'm a tram!'

There's a wonderful family called Stein,
There's Gert and there's Ep and there's Ein;
  Gert's poems are bunk,
  Ep's statues are junk,
And no-one can understand Ein.

There was a young fellow called Willie
Whose behaviour was frequently silly.
  At a big UNO ball,
  Dressed in nothing at all,
He claimed that his costume was Chile.

There was a young lady named Bright,
Who travelled much faster than light.
  She started one day
  In the relative way
And returned on the previous night.

There was a faith-healer of Deal,
Who said, 'Although pain isn't real,
  If I sit on a pin
  And it punctures my skin,
I dislike what I fancy I feel.'

There was an old man from Nantucket,
Who kept all his cash in a bucket.
  His daughter, named Nan,
  Ran away with a man,
And as for the bucket, Nantucket.

A colonel called out with great force
In the midst of Hyde Park for a horse.
  All the soldiers looked round,
  But none could be found:
So he just rhododendron. Of course.

2. Try your hand at writing limericks.

HAIKU

Haiku is a Japanese word for a short poem of seventeen syllables arranged in three lines: five syllables in the first line, seven in the second and five in the third. The haiku is one of the traditional Japanese poetic forms and it reached a peak of excellence in the eighteenth century. It was not simply a question of counting syllables, however. The haiku was expected to observe certain rules of composition which made it a more difficult art form than its three lines might suggest. The seventeen syllables were not only arranged in a 5 — 7 — 5 sequence; they were expected to end with a noun or a strongly emotional word also. In addition, each haiku had to contain a word or a phrase referring to one of the four seasons. Thus, spring might be suggested by cherry blossom, summer by cicadas, autumn by the harvest moon and winter by a cold shower of rain.

Bashō, one of the great Japanese poets of the eighteenth century, asserted that haiku should be rooted in everyday life, yet should not be expressed in colloquial language; the poet should 'mingle with the herd, yet preserve a noble mind.' The individual haiku should describe a particular incident and at the same time suggest a universal principle. Bashō's most famous haiku illustrates this:

An old pond
A frog jumps in —
Sound of water.

The pond represents the permanence of the world, the unchanging, the passive; the jump of the frog symbolises the active force in life, occurring in the moment only and therefore impermanent; the splash represents the interaction of the two, the fusion of the momentary with the timeless.

Not all Japanese poets, however, thought haiku ought to be based on such a subtle philosophical equation and many who followed Bashō deliberately avoided symbolism and brought the haiku down to a more personal and realistic level. 'Be natural, 'said one poet, 'prefer real pictures.' This 'naturalism' led, in the twentieth century, to a movement away from the disciplines of classical haiku towards a freer expression in which the syllable-count was often abandoned and a much more colloquial style of language introduced.

Haiku were introduced into Europe about the turn of the century and they caught on particularly in France, where a literary magazine promoted a haiku competition and attracted over a thousand entries. In England the haiku has been a popular form of poetry for a great many years now, though the 5 — 7 — 5 syllable-pattern has not always been strictly followed and the poem has tended to become a simple three-line verse of comment or observation. Rather like a snapshot, it captures a living moment and shows that the poet has observed some detail or quality of a scene which he records with an accuracy and insight that bring it alive in the reader's mind. Usually the first two lines act as the statement and the final line becomes a conclusion. There is a satisfying neatness about a good haiku, and yet it doesn't say everything — it leaves the reader to add a thought himself and to pick up the implications of what has been said:

> When dawn breaks
> The fire-fly
> Becomes an insect.

The haiku, for all its simplicity of construction, can cover a wide variety of subjects and is particularly effective at portraying a natural scene:

> The first snow,
> Just enough to bend
> The leaves of the daffodils.

— and at showing an insight into human nature:

> Lying with arms and legs outstretched,
> How cool, —
> How lonely!

Very often there is a nice touch of humour:

> Under his very feet
> The beans are being stolen, —
> What a scarecrow!

These haiku are translations from the Japanese and do not, therefore, represent English poetry; yet the haiku has become so well-established in this country — particularly in schools, where it is often used as an introduction to the writing of poetry — that it deserves to be studied as one of the new English poetic forms.

1   In the haiku below the poet leaves something to the imagination and understanding of the reader through implying more than he states. Can you say what this is?

Tilling the field,
The cloud that never moved
Is gone

Buson

The cherry blossom having fallen,
Enjoji temple
Is quiet once more.

Onitsura

Sweeping them up,
And then not sweeping them up,
The falling leaves.

Taigi

2. Which of the following haiku seem to you to contain:
a) a sharp observation of nature;
b) an insight into human nature?

This ramshackle house,
And me just the same as ever, —
The first day of spring.

Issa

Baby mice in their nest
Squeak in response
To the young sparrows.

Bashō

Crawl — and laugh!
From today
You are two!

Issa

Clearing up in the evening;
In the pale blue sky;
Row upon row of autumn mountains.

Issa

The wren
Looking here, looking there —
"Dropped something?"

Issa

Foxes playing
Among the narcissus flowers;
A bright moonlit night.

Buson

The kingfisher;
On its wet feathers
Shines the evening sun.

Tôri

O flea!
Don't jump whatever you do —
That way is the River Sumida.

Issa

On a withered branch,
A crow is perched
In the autumn evening.

Killing flies,
I begin to wish
To annihilate them all.

Bisho

Seibi

In my mid-day nap,
I hear the song of the rice-planters,
And feel somewhat ashamed of myself.

Issa

For my sake,
Do not light the lamp yet,
This evening of spring.

Gyodai

3. Which of the haiku quoted in this chapter seem to you to contain an interesting use of figurative language?

4. Writing haiku can be an easy and enjoyable introduction to the writing of poetry. Having studied the form and style of Japanese haiku, you may be prepared to write some haiku of your own, based on your observation of people and the world around you. Forget about the 5 — 7 — 5 syllable count to start with — simply 'be natural — prefer real pictures'.

PARODY

There is a danger that poetry will be taken too seriously. There has to be a safety-valve, a way of putting poetry in its place and laughing at it, instead of treating it as though it *mattered*. After all, as the American poet Marianne Moore observed in her poem, *Poetry*:

> I, too, dislike it; there are things that are important beyond all this fiddle.

There has developed in poetry, therefore, as well as in other forms of literature, the art of comic imitation. It is called *parody* and it aims at imitating a serious original and making fun of it. The parody is close enough in form and style to the original to be a recognisable imitation, but the parodist replaces the seriousness with humour and exaggeration. For parody to work successfully one ought to know what is being parodied, but many parodies have outclassed their originals and are popular in their own right.

Parody probably begins in childhood for most people, for children are not unnaturally keen on making up comic, often rude, versions of songs, hymns and carols that they are expected to take seriously in certain places. *The Lore and Language of Schoolchildren* quotes several examples of children's parody, much of it still part of the oral tradition of street and playground. There are numerous versions of *Mary had a little lamb*, for instance; several of *The boy stood on the burning deck*; and at least one for each of the poplular Christmas carols, like this version of *Good King Wenceslas*:

> Good King Wenceslas looked out
> On the Feast of Stephen;
> A snowball hit him on the snout
> And made it all uneven.
> Brightly shone his conk that night
> Though the pain was cruel,
> Till the doctor came in sight
> Riding on a mu-oo-el

It is a perfect example of parody — starting off in all apparent seriousness with the opening words of the original, then plunging abruptly into the ridiculous in the third line and continuing to the end of the verse, yet still keeping pace with the original metre and altering the rhyme only to introduce the comic word *snout* and to pair-off — very cleverly — *cruel* and *mu-oo-el* (mule).

One of the great parodists in English poetry was Lewis Carroll, who took little moral Victorian verses and turned them into comic poems which then became part of the greater parody which is *Alice in Wonderland*. There is, for instance, a well-intentioned poem by G W Langford called *Speak Gently*, which begins with the verse:

> Speak gently; it is better far
> To rule by love than fear;
> Speak gently; let no harsh word mar
> The good we may do here.

In *Alice in Wonderland* these high-minded sentiments are parodied to become:

> Speak roughly to your little boy,
> And beat him when he sneezes;
> He only does it to annoy,
> Because he knows it teases.

Another example of Lewis Carroll's turning sentimental piety on its head is in his parody of *Star of Evening*, by James M Sayles:

> BEAU-TI-FUL STAR in heav'n so bright,
> Soft-ly falls thy sil-v'ry light,
> As thou mov-est from earth a-far,
> Star of the eve-ning, beau-ti-ful star,
> Star of the eve-ning, beau-ti-ful star.
>
> Chorus:
> > Beau-ti-ful star, —
> > Beau-ti-ful star, —
> > Star — of the eve-ning,
> > Beau-ti-ful, beau-ti-ful star . . ..
>
> Shine on, oh star of love divine,
> And may our soul's affections twine
> Around thee as thou movest afar,
> Star of the twilight, beautiful star.

In *Alice in Wonderland* this becomes:

> BEAUTIFUL SOUP, so rich and green,
> Waiting in a hot tureen!
> Who for such dainties would not stoop?
> Soup of the evening, beautiful Soup!
> Soup of the evening, beautiful Soup!

Beau-ootiful Soo-oop!
Beau-ootiful Soo-oop!
Soo-oop of the e-e-evening,
Beautiful, beautiful Soup!

Beautiful Soup! who cares for fish,
Game, or any other dish?
Who would not give all else for two p
ennyworth only of beautiful Soup?
Pennyworth only of beautiful Soup?
Pennyworth only of beautiful Soup?
Beau-ootiful Soo-oop!
Beau-ootiful Soo-oop!
Soo-oop of the e-e-evening
Beautiful, beauti-FUL SOUP!

Here Lewis Carroll is obviously imitating the first poem: the
structure is almost identical, with a verse of four-stress metre
followed by a chorus (though the parody adds a line in the second
verse to create a balance with the first). The language is a direct
echo, with the repetitions of *beautiful* and *evening*, as well as the
breaking down into syllables of *beau-ootiful Soo-oop*, the long
'oo's' suggesting the expression of real delight that children might
take in the soup. What makes the parody effective, however, is the
change in subject from the 'poetic' star of evening to the very
ordinary and unpoetic tureen of soup. Lewis Carroll, through his
mimicry, is laughing at the sentimentality that lavishes love on
the remote evening star when we might more sensibly turn our
praise to something more substantial and accessible, like the rich
green soup! In place of the pious sentiment:

And may our soul's affections twine
Around thee as thou movest afar,

he asks a simple homely question:

Who would not give all else for two p
ennyworth only of beautiful soup?

He probably felt that at least we know where we are when we talk
of beautiful soup, whereas to address our affections to the evening
star is to become dangerously lost in fancy. Above all, however, he
makes the parody funny and he demonstrates that humorous
imitation is one of the most enjoyable forms of verse.

1. Read the following poems and answer the questions on them.

The Burial of Sir John Moore at Corunna commemorates the

eminent soldier's death in the Napoleonic Wars and was written by
a young curate, Charles Wolfe, who wrote nothing else of note. It
was published in 1817 and its popularity lasted well into the
twentieth century.

Not a Sous Has He Got is a parody of the first poem and was
written by E H Barham (1788-1845), a clergyman with a gift for
satirical imitation.

The Burial of Sir John Moore at Corunna

Not a drum was heard, not a funeral note,
　　As his corpse to the rampart we hurried;
Not a soldier discharged his farewell shot
　　O'er the grave where our hero we buried.

We buried him darkly at dead of night,
　　The sods with our bayonets turning;
By the struggling moonbeam's misty light
　　And the lantern dimly burning.

No useless coffin enclosed his breast,
　　Not in sheet nor in shroud we wound him;
But he lay like a warrior taking his rest,
　　With his martial cloak around him.

Few and short were the prayers we said,
　　And we spoke not a word of sorrow;
But we steadfastly gazed on the face that was dead,
　　And we bitterly thought of the morrow.

We thought, as we hollow'd his narrow bed
　　And smoothed down his lonely pillow,
That the foe and the stranger would tread o'er his head,
　　And we far away on the billow!

Lightly they'll talk of the spirit that's gone
　　And o'er his cold ashes upbraid him, —
But little he'll reck, if they let him sleep on
　　In the grave where a Briton has laid him.

But half of our heavy task was done
　　When the clock struck the hour for retiring:
And we heard the distant and random gun
　　That the foe was sullenly firing.

Slowly and sadly we laid him down,
　　From the field of his fame fresh and gory;
We carved not a line, and we raised not a stone —
　　But we left him alone with his glory.

C Wolfe

Not a Sous Had He Got

Not a sous had he got, — not a guinea nor note,
    And he looked confoundedly flurried,
As he bolted away without paying his shot,
    And the Landlady after him hurried.

We saw him again at dead of night,
    When home from the Club returning;
We twigg'd the Doctor beneath the light
    Of the gas-lamp brilliantly burning.

All bare, and exposed to the midnight dews,
    Reclined in the gutter we found him;
And he looked like a gentleman taking a snooze,
    With his *Marshall* cloak around him.

'The Doctor's as drunk as the d . . . . ,' we said,
    And we managed a shutter to borrow;
We raised him, and sigh'd at the thought that his head
    Would consumedly ache on the morrow.

We bore him home, and we put him to bed,
    And we told his wife and his daughter
To give him, next morning, a couple of red
    Herrings, with soda-water.

Loudly they talk'd of his money that's gone,
    And his Lady began to upbraid him;
But little he reck'd, so they let him snooze on
    'Neath the counterpane just as we laid him.

We tucked him in, and had hardly done
    When, beneath the window calling,
We heard the rough voice of a son of a gun
    Of a watchman 'One of clock' bawling.

Slowly and sadly we all walked down
    From his room in the uppermost story;
A rushlight we placed on the cold hearth-stone,
    And we left him alone in his glory.

R H Barham

a) Compare the verse form of both poems. How closely does the
rhyme of the parody follow the rhyme of the original?

b) What is the equivalent in the parody of these lines in *The Burial?*
  i) *And the lantern dimly burning;*
  ii) *But he lay like a warrior taking his rest;*
  iii) *Few and short were the prayers we said;*
  iv) *Lightly they'll talk of the spirit that's gone;*
  v) *In the grave where a Briton has laid him;*
  vi) *And we heard the distant and random gun*
      That the foe was sullenly firing.

c) *The Burial* describes the secrecy and simplicity of the funeral of a great soldier on whom considerable honour would have been bestowed if he had died in England. What details in the poem stress: i) the secrecy; ii) the simplicity of his burial?

d) What feelings of reverence for the 'hero' are expressed?

e) What reasons probably prompted R H Barham to parody *The Burial?*

f) Is the parody an amusing poem in its own right, or does its humour depend on a reader knowing the original? Give your reasons.

g) Which of these poems do you prefer? Explain your choice.

2. Parody with a serious purpose is rare. Paul Dehn bases his on nursery rhyme and hymn, but he is making a serous comment. Explain what it is.

a)   Ring-a-ring o' neutrons,
        A pocketful of positrons,
        A fission! A fission!
        We all fall down.

b)   The day God gave thee, Man, is ending;
            The darkness falls at thy behest,
        Who spent thy little life defending
            (From conquest by the East) the West.

        The sun, that bids us live, is waking
            Behind the cloud that bids us die,
        And in the murk fresh minds are making
            New plans to blow us all sky-high.

c)   "Mary, Mary, quite contrary,
            Say how the bomb test went."
        "I'll let you know in a week or so,
            When I've had my Happy Event."

For a further study of parody, read: *The Song of Wandering Aengus* by W B Yeats and *The Hero* by Roger Woddis (pages 117– 118).

CONCRETE POETRY

Poetry can make a visual impact upon us. When we look at the page with the poem printed on it we see certain shapes — perhaps rectangles of print consisting of lines of more-or-less equal length; or solid columns running down the centre of the page; or paragraphs that sprawl about irregularly. In all this, however, the poet is simply following a recognised verse form, such as the ballad, blank verse or free verse; the shape of the poem on the page has no particular meaning. That, however, was before the arrival of 'concrete' poetry, a movement that started in the 1950's in both Brazil and Germany and which has since spread more widely.

The aim of the 'concrete' poets is to make use of the arrangement of letters, words and sentences on the page to produce a visual meaning that links up with what the words themselves are expressing. However, it is not merely a typographical trick in which the poem is printed in imitation of the shape of an object. It goes further than this. Occasionally there are no words at all — simply letters. Often there is no statement that makes literal sense, or there is just a pattern of repetition; but the poet is implying a meaning or eliciting a response through the arrangement of the type on the page. It is rather like combining the art of typography with the art of poetry. Concrete poetry can be serious and comic, simple or complex, lucid or obscure — much as any other poetry can be and it has opened up a whole new field of poetic expression.

Though Roger McGough was not part of the concrete-poetry movement, his poem, *40 — Love* is concrete in character:

middle	aged
couple	playing
ten-	nis
when	the
game	ends
and	they
go	home
the	net
will	still
be	be-
tween	them

In what way is the arrangement of the words on the page linked with the subject of the poem? It is not difficult to see that the movement of your eyes from one side of the page to the other imitates the movement of the ball from one side of the tennis court to the other. The gap in the middle represents the gap in the relationship between the middle-aged man and his wife. It is there, with the net separating them on the tennis court, and it is there psychologically when they return home after the game. What do you make of the title of the poem?

E E Cummings's poem *Grasshopper* is an intriguing exercise in concrete form and takes a bit of puzzling out:

<pre>
                                    r-p-o-p-h-e-s-s-a-g-r
                          who
            a)s w(e loo)k
            upnowgath
                        PPEGORHRASS
                                        eringint(o-
            aThe):l
                  eA
                     !p:
         S   a
                          (r
            rIvInG   .gRrEaPsPhOs)
                                              to
            rea(be)rran(com)gi(e)ngly
            ,grasshopper;
</pre>

The idea is that the grasshopper leaps up into the air and comes down again; but he seems to change shape with each stage of the process and this is represented in the poem by the letters of *grasshopper* being made into anagrams: first r-p-o-p-h-e-s-s-a-g-r, then PPEGORHRASS, then, as he lands, gRrEaPsPhOs, and finally *grasshopper* again. The rest of the poem is fairly straightforward if one separates the words that have been joined together and joins the words that have been separated. It now reads (omitting the anagrams):

who as we look up now gathering into . . . (g)athe(ring):
leaps! arriving to become rearrangingly grasshopper.

It is one way of describing the jump of the grasshopper and it can be argued that it is at least as good as the conventional poetic way.

1. Comment on the following poem by Eugen Gomringer:

> silence silence silence
> silence silence silence
> silence   silence
> silence silence silence
> silence silence silence

2. *Near the Guernsey Coast*

gulls   bulls

boats   goats

Dom Sylvesteer Houedard

a) What do you know through the arrangement of the words on the page that you would not have known if the words had been arranged in another way?
b) What reason is there for calling this arrangement of words a 'poem'?

3.   *Reflection*

When you look	kool uoy nehW
into a mirror	rorrim a otni
it is not	ton si ti
yourself you see,	,ees uoy flesruoy
but a kind	dnik a tub
of apish error	rorre hsipa fo
posed in fearful	lufraef ni desop
symmetry.	.yrtemmys

John Updike

a) What typographical technique is the poet using here?
b) Is the difference between the two halves of the poem greater or less than the difference between a real face and its reflection in a mirror?

4. Comment on the following concrete poem by Eugen
Gomringer:

```
                              o
                              bo
                              blow
                              blow blow
                              blow blow blow
                              blow blow
                              blow
                              bo
            o                 o
            go                so
            grow              show
            grow grow         show show
            grow grow grow o show show show
            grow grow         show show
            grow              show
            go                so
            o                 o
            lo
            flo
      flow flow
   flow flow flow
      flow flow
            flow
            lo
            o
```

FOUND POETRY

Some people are poets without knowing it! This is not to say that they speak in rhyme all the time, but that they speak or write in a way that contains some of the basic elements of poetry, such as rhythm, metaphor, imagery and a pattern of statements. When Alfred Doolittle in *Pygmalion* says: 'I'm waiting to tell you, I'm wanting to tell you, I'm willing to tell you', we can immediately recognise something poetic in the rhythm and the repetition of his speech. The same is true of much that is written in books on non-literary subjects, in catalogues, in personal letters, in lists of contents, on labels, on public notices — there is no saying where you might not find a piece of writing which in its structure and its use of language resembles poetry.

The name given to this spontaneous and accidental poetry is *found* poetry and it is open to anyone to find examples of it. There is certainly a pleasure in discovering in language quite unconnected with poetry some of the imagination, feeling and verbal pattern that poetry contains; but it is also interesting to use found poetry as an exercise in critical analysis, for in deciding whether or not a piece of 'ordinary' writing is poetic or not, one is really asking the question: 'What constitutes poetry?' A study of found poetry, therefore, can help to define the criteria by which we judge the more orthodox forms of poetry.

The first example is from *The Concise Oxford Dictionary of Music*.

Value of Notes

1 Semibreve	equals	1 Whole-note
2 Minims	or	2 Half-notes
4 Crotchets	or	4 Quarter-notes
8 Quavers	or	8 Eighth-notes
16 Semiquavers	or	16 Sixteenth-notes
32 Demisemiquavers	or	32 Thirty-second notes

After this follow hemidemisemiquavers (sixty-fourth notes)
And occasionally semihemidemisemiquavers (notes of 128 to the
  semibreve)

It is easy to see the pattern made by the table: the balance of the statements on the two sides, with the 'equals' and the 'or' acting as pivots. Then there is the development of the numbers, doubling each time until the last two lines when the balance and rhythm are dropped for the more direct statement. The two long

97

words 'hemidemisemiquavers' and 'semihemidemisemiquavers'
provide a multiple-rhyme climax to the progression. Read aloud, I
think it would sound unmistakably rhythmical, like verse based on
a metrical system; and though written without a poetic intention,
it nevertheless contains a recognisable echo of poetic technique.

The second example of found poetry is taken from The
Reader's Digest *Book of British Birds.* It describes the habits and
movements of birds in South Wales during each month of the year.

Pick of the Year

JANUARY:	ravens flock to communal tree-roosts in Cardiganshire and Brecknock
FEBRUARY:	buzzards and ravens roam the hills, often competing for the carcasses of dead sheep
MARCH:	buzzards begin to build their large stick nests in trees or on ledges
APRIL:	gannets on Grassholme
MAY:	wood warblers in the hill woods
JUNE:	pied flycatchers and young buzzards make their first, unsteady flights
JULY:	young choughs leave their island breeding-grounds and visit the Pembrokeshire coasts in family parties
AUGUST:	Manx sheerwaters tend their chicks in nest burrows on the islands of Skokholm and Skomer
SEPTEMBER:	migrant warblers and chats are numerous on the coast and islands of Pembrokeshire
OCTOBER:	flocks of migrant thrushes and larks, bound for wintering grounds in southern Ireland, can be seen on Skokholm and Skomer
NOVEMBER:	winter roosts of rooks and jackdaws in farming areas
DECEMBER:	vast flocks of oystercatchers winter near Whiteford Burrows.

What have we got that resembles poetry? The subject, first of
all, is traditionally a subject of English poetry — the observation of
nature. Many of the phrases might have come from a 'real' poem:
buzzards and ravens roam the hills for instance; whilst *competing
for the carcasses of dead sheep* conjures up a vivid picture of the
fierce rivalry of the famished birds. There is also a comic touch in
the line: *young choughs leave their island breeding grounds and
visit the Pembrokeshire coast in family parties.* The assonance in
roosts of rooks and in *pied flycatchers* has the effect of subdued
rhyme and the alliteration that occurs throughout in phrases like

gannets on Grassholme, wood warblers in hill woods, seen on Skokholm and Skomer and *winter near Whiteford* gives the piece a musical quality that is not often found in prose. Moreover, just as the structure of a poem can be made up of a series of stanzas, so this piece of writing finds its structure in the months of the year.

What needs to be remembered in discussing found poetry, however, is that it hardly ever contains all the elements of poetry. There may be a technical similarity, such as rhythm, alliteration and figurative language; there may be poetic thought and feeling, but there is unlikely to be meaning shaped into expression by the poet's craft, which is the sign of intentional, rather than found, poetry.

Below are some examples of found poetry. What comments can you make about their poetic content?

1. Pronunciation of Indian words, from *The Art and Architecture of India.*

a	as in America
a	as in father
e	always long, as in late
i	as in bit
i	as in **eel**
o	always long, as in note
u	as in foot
u	as in boot
bh	as in **cab-horse**
c	as in **church**
ch	as in **church-house**
dh	as in **mad-house**
n or m	as in **sing**
ph	as in **uphill**
th	as in **anthill**

2. From *The Oxford Book of Music:* Time Signatures.

Simple Duple
Compound Duple
Simple Triple
Compound Triple
Simple Quadruple
Compound Quadruple

3. From Dryad Handicrafts' Catalogue: Dryad Brushes.

> WATER COLOUR BRUSHES. Best quality bear hair in
> aluminium ferrules on polished handles.
> SABLE BRUSHES. Selected pure red sable in plated brass
> ferrules on black polished handles.
> ROUND HOG BRUSHES. For use with powder colours. Best
> white bristle in plated brass ferrules on long polished handles.
> FLAT HOG BRUSHES. For use with powder colours. Best
> white bristle in plated brass ferrules on long polished handles.
> OIL COLOUR BRUSHES. Flat filbert shape, finest hog hair
> in plated ferrules on long polished handles.

4. Find some examples of found poetry.

POEMS FOR CLOSER STUDY

Counting the Beats

You, love, and I,
(He whispers) you and I,
And if no more than only you and I
What care you or I?

Counting the beats,
Counting the slow heart beats,
The bleeding to death of time in slow heart beats,
Wakeful they lie.

Cloudless day,
Night, and a cloudless day,
Yet the huge storm will burst upon their heads one day
From a bitter sky.

Where shall we be,
(She whispers) where shall we be,
When death strikes home, O where then shall we be
Who were you and I?

Not there but here,
(He whispers) only here,
As we are, here together, now and here,
Always you and I.

Counting the beats,
Counting the slow heart beats,
The bleeding to death of time in slow heart beats,
Wakeful they lie.

Robert Graves

1. Count the beats in each line of the poem. What pattern
   emerges?
2. Study the rhythm that results from the metrical beats. What
   rhythm is Robert Graves imitating?
3. The third line of each verse is much longer than the rest. What
   effect is being aimed at?
4. What question worries the girl?
5. What reassurance does the young man give her?
6. What is the poet saying in the third verse about the future of
   the lovers?

7. The final verse is a repetition of the second verse and ends on the phrase *wakeful they lie.* What is implied by the word *wakeful?*
8. What do you think of Robert Graves's view of love in the poem?
9. What have you found effective in his poetic technique?

The Labourer

There he goes, tacking against the fields'
Uneasy tides. What have the centuries done
To change him? The same garments, frayed with light
Or seamed with rain, cling to the wind-scoured bones
And shame him in the eyes of the spruce birds.
Once it was ignorance, then need, but now
Habit that drapes him on a bush of cloud
For life to mock at, while the noisy surf
Of people dins far off at the world's rim.
He has been here since life began, a vague
Movement among the roots of the young grass.
Bend down and peer beneath the twigs of hair,
And look into the hard eyes, flecked with care;
What do you see? Notice the twitching hands,
Veined like a leaf, and tough bark of the limbs,
Wrinkled and gnarled, and tell me what you think.
A wild tree still, whose seasons are not yours,
The slow heart beating to the hidden pulse,
Of the strong sap, the feet firm in the soil?
No, no, a man like you, but blind with tears
Of sweat to the bright star that draws you on.

R S Thomas

1. Quote from the poem to show that R S Thomas is referring to a type of person rather than an individual.
2. The labourer is described as:
   ....*tacking against the fields'*
   Uneasy tides.

   What exactly is he doing? Where is this metaphor taken up later in the poem?
3. The labourer can be thought of as *a wild tree.* How is this metaphor used more specifically in the second part of the poem?

4. What gives R S Thomas such regret about the life of the labourer?
5. He says: *No, no, a man like you, but . . .* What, in your own words, is the difference between the labourer and the 'ordinary' man?

Sunken Evening

The green light floods the city square —
    A sea of fowl and feathered fish,
    Where squalls of rainbirds dive and splash
And gusty sparrows chop the air.

Submerged, the prawn-blue pigeons feed
    In sandy grottoes round the Mall,
    And crusted lobster-buses crawl
Among the fountains' silver weed.

There, like a wreck, with mast and bell,
    The torn church settles by the bow,
    While phosphorescent starlings stow
Their mussel shells along the hull.

The oyster-poet, drowned but dry,
    Rolls a black pearl between his bones;
    The typist, trapped by telephones,
Gazes in bubbles at the sky.

Till, with the dark, the shallows run,
    And homeward surges tide and fret —
    The slow night trawls its heavy net
And hauls the clerk to Surbiton.

Laurie Lee

1. What is the significance of the title of the poem?
2. What underwater connection does Laurie Lee establish metaphorically with: the evening light; the pigeons; the buses; the church; the starlings; the typist; the journey to the suburbs in the evening?
3. What is the *black pearl* that the oyster-poet is in process of creating?
4. Comment on the rhyme.
5. What merits do you think this poem has? Have you any criticism to make of it?

The Edge of Day

The dawn's precise pronouncement waits
With breath of light indrawn,
Then forms with smoky, smut-red lips
The great O of the sun.

The mouldering atoms of the dark
Blaze into morning air;
The birdlike stars droop down and die,
The starlike birds catch fire.

The thrush's tinder throat strikes up,
The sparrow chips hot sparks
From flinty tongue, and all the sky
Showers with electric larks.

And my huge eye a chaos is
Where molten worlds are born;
Where floats the eagle's flaming moon,
And crows, like clinkers, burn;

Where blackbirds scream with comet tails,
And flaring finches fall,
And starlings, aimed like meteors,
Bounce from the garden wall;

Where, from the edge of day I spring
Alive for mortal flight,
Lit by the heart's exploding sun
Bursting from night to night.

Laurie Lee

1. What, in literal terms, is being described in the first verse?
    What figure of speech has Laurie Lee used in his description?
2. As you read through the poem you realise that the metaphors
    used to describe the birds are all linked to a theme. What is
    this theme? What has it to do with the beginning of the day?
    Quote these metaphors and underline the words in them that
    have a thematic connection.
3. What is your opinion of the metaphorical descriptions? Do
    they bring the scene alive and help you to imagine the
    movements and appearance of the birds? Are they contrived
    and exaggerated — the poet showing off his poetic skill rather
    than revealing the birds' true nature? A justified use of
    hyperbole to express the poet's heightened feelings of wonder

and joy? Quote examples from the poem to support your
point of view.
4. Do you detect two puns in the third verse?
5. What is Laurie Lee saying about himself in the final verse?
6. What reasons are there for thinking that the scene that is
described in the poem is either real or imaginary?

Ears in the Turrets Hear

Ears in the turrets hear
Hands grumble on the door,
Eyes in the gables see
The fingers at the locks.
Shall I unbolt or stay
Alone till the day I die
Unseen by stranger-eyes
In this white house?
Hands, hold you poison or grapes?

Beyond this island bound
By a thin sea of flesh
And a bone coast,
The land lies out of sound
And the hills out of mind.
No birds or flying fish
Disturbs this island's rest.

Ears in this island hear
The wind pass like a fire,
Eyes in this island see
Ships anchor off the bay.
Shall I run to the ships
With the wind in my hair,
Or stay till the day I die
And welcome no sailor?
Ships, hold you poison or grapes?

Hands grumble on the door,
Ships anchor off the bay,
Rain beats the sand and slates.
Shall I let in the stranger,
Shall I welcome the sailor,
Or stay till the day I die?

Hands of the stranger and holds of the ships,
Hold you poison or grapes?

Dylan Thomas

1. The woman who is the subject of the poem is seen in metaphorical terms. Trace the use of this metaphor throughout the poem.
2. Why is it appropriate to depict the house as *white?*
3. How is the idea of intrusion into the woman's privacy depicted?
4. Comment on the word *grumbles.*
5. The woman's dilemma is expressed in the questions she asks herself. Using the language of the poem, say what alternatives are open to her?
6. The woman's doubts arise from her indecision about giving up her isolation. She asks: *Hands, hold you poison or grapes?* What do these words symbolise in her mind?

From *Morte d'Arthur*

Then saw they how there hove a dusky barge,
Dark as a funeral scarf from stem to stern,
Beneath them; and descending they were ware
That all the decks were dense with stately forms
Black-stoled, black-hooded, like a dream — by these
Three Queens with crowns of gold — and from them rose
A cry that shiver'd to the tingling stars,
And, as it were one voice, an agony
Of lamentation, like a wind, that shrills
All night in a waste land, where no one comes,
Or hath come, since the making of the world.
Then murmur'd Arthur, 'Place me in the barge,'
And to the barge they came. There those three Queens
Put forth their hands, and took the King, and wept.
But she, that rose the tallest of them all
And fairest, laid his head upon her lap,
And loosed the shatter'd casque, and chafed his hands,
And call'd him by his name, complaining loud,
And dropping bitter tears against his brow
Striped with dark blood: for all his face was white
And colourless, and like the wither'd moon
Smote by the fresh beam of the springing east;
And all his greaves and cuisses dash'd with drops
Of onset; and the light and lustrous curls—
That made his forehead like a rising sun
High from the dais-throne— were parch'd with dust;
Or, clotted into points and hanging loose,

Mix'd with the knightly growth that fringed his lips.
So like a shatter'd column lay the King;
Not like that Arthur who, with lance in rest,
From spur to plume a star of tournament,
Shot thro' the lists at Camelot, and charged
Before the eyes of ladies and of kings.

Lord Tennyson

The dying Arthur has been carried by Sir Bedivere to the lake
where a barge is waiting.
1. What is appropriate about describing the barge as being *dark as
    a funeral scarf?*
2. *Like a dream* suggests the mystery, the unreality of the three
    black-stoled figures in the barge. What impression is Tennyson
    trying to convey through the simile beginning, *like a
    wind . . . ?*
3. Which two similes seem intended as a contrast to each other —
    one depicting the dying Arthur, the other the young king?
4. What is suggested about Arthur's former greatness in the
    simile, *like a shattered column?*
5. Tennyson seems to be deliberately contrasting the aged,
    wounded Arthur with the man as he was at the height of his
    powers. Quote some details to show how he does this.
6. Show by quotation what mood Tennyson creates in the
    passage.

From *Skylarks*

I

The lark begins to go up
Like a warning
As if the globe were uneasy —

Barrell-chested for heights,
Like an Indian of the high Andes,

A whippet head, barbed like a hunting arrow,

But leaden
With muscle
For the struggle
Against
Earth's centre.

And leaden
For ballast
In the rocketing storms of the breath.

Leaden
Like a bullet
To supplant
Life from its centre.

II

Crueller than owl or eagle

A towered bird, shot through the crested head
With the command, Not die

But climb

Climb

Sing

Obedient as to death a dead thing.

III

I suppose you just gape and let your gaspings
Rip in and out through your voicebox
                              O lark

And sing inwards as well as outwards
Like a breaker of ocean milling the shingle
                              O lark

O song, incomprehensively both ways —
Joy! Help! Joy! Help!
                    O lark

IV

You stop to rest, far up, you teeter
Over the drop

But not stopping singing

Resting only for a second

Dropping just a little

Then up and up and up

Like a mouse with drowning fur
Bobbing and bobbing at the well-wall

Lamenting, mounting a little —

But the sun will not take notice
And the earth's centre smiles.

V

My idleness curdles
Seeing the lark labour near its cloud
Scrambling
In a nightmare difficulty
Up through the nothing

Its feathers thrash, its heart must be drumming like a motor,
As if it were too late, too late

Dithering in ether
Its song whirls faster and faster
And the sun whirls
The lark is evaporating
Till my eye's gossamer snaps
                and my hearing floats back widely to earth

After which the sky lies blank open
Without wings, and the earth is a folded clod.

Only the sun goes silently and endlessly on with the lark's
        song.

Ted Hughes

1. The poem is written in free verse, yet the lines and verses are
   arranged with a particular effect in mind. Choose some
   examples from the poem of arrangements of lines and verses
   that are designed to create a particular effect.
2. Similes are used to describe the bird. What qualities in the
   skylark do the similes in the first section of the poem
   emphasise? Are all these similes convincing in the comparisons
   which they suggest?
3. What rhythmic effects do you find in the poem?
4. There are several examples of onomatopoeia. Can you quote
   them?
5. Explain why:
           . . . the sun will not take notice
           And the earth's centre smiles.
6. What is Ted Hughes feeling when he writes:
       My idleness curdles
       Seeing the lark labour near its cloud

7. What is meant by . . . *my eye's gossamer snaps?*
8. Put together in quotation what Ted Hughes is saying about the skylark, then say: a) what impresses him about the bird; b) how realistic and convincing a portrait it is of the bird.

The Last Laugh

'O Jesus Christ! I'm hit,' he said; and died.
Whether he vainly cursed, or prayed indeed,
The Bullets chirped — In vain! vain! vain!
Machine-guns chuckled, 'Tut-tut! Tut-tut!
And the Big Gun guffawed.

Another sighed, — O Mother, Mother! Dad!'
Then smiled, at nothing, childlike, being dead.
    And the lofty Shrapnel-cloud
    Leisurely gestured, — Fool!
    And the falling splinters tittered.

'My Love!' one moaned. Love-languid seemed his mood,
Till, slowly lowered, his whole face kissed the mud.
    And the Bayonets' long teeth grinned;
    Rabbles of Shells hooted and groaned;
    And the Gas hissed.

Wilfred Owen

1. Show how the subjects of the three verses are almost identical. What slight variations are there?
2. What attitude to the deaths of the soldiers does Wilfred Owen attribute to the weapons through the personifications? Quote some examples.
3. We know that weapons such as bullets and bayonets are inanimate and therefore have no feelings about the deaths they cause. Does this make nonsense of the poem? Can you suggest what Wilfred Owen in saying *in fact* about war through the personifications in the poem?
4. Can you see anything grimly ironical in the word *childlike* (line 7) and in the phrase *kissed the mud* (line 12)?
5. What use is made of onomatopoeia in the poem?
6. What type of rhyme is used in the poem? Is the use of rhyme linked to the subject matter of each verse? What is the total effect of the rhyme — or absence of it — in the poem?
7. What is the point being made in the title?
8. Are your feelings about war affected by reading the poem?

Discord in Childhood

Outside the house an ash-tree hung its terrible whips,
And at night when the wind rose, the lash of the tree
Shrieked and slashed the wind, as a ship's
Weird rigging in a storm shrieks hideously.

Within the house two voices arose, a slender lash
Whistling she-delirious rage, and the dreadful sound
Of a male thong booming and bruising, until it had drowned
The other voice in a silence of blood, 'neath the noise of the
ash.

D H Lawrence

1. Say briefly what each stanza is concerned with.
2. What figurative expressions are used in the first stanza to describe the movements of the branches of the tree in the wind?
3. What parallels have these expressions in the second stanza?
4. Consider the simile in the first stanza. Is it an effective reinforcement of the metaphors already used? Or does it seem inappropriate to introduce a nautical comparison into the poem?
5. Lawrence wishes to describe the two voices in argument and he does this by a subtle use of alliteration and onomatopoeia added to metaphor. Explain how he uses these effects to suggest the sound of: a) the woman's voice; b) the man's voice.
6. What idea connects the words *lash* and *thong?* What is suggested in the relationship of the man and the woman by use of these two words?
7. What, literally, has happened in the second stanza?
8. What is added to the poem by the title?

The Tomb of David Hume

The Trifid Nebula to my green eyes
Looks like an aged pundit gazing down
At worlds of mortals; I see a frown
And tilted head and folded hands; a wise

Old meditating gentleman who tries
To do his best but gets weary. A crown
Of stars suspended to his left; a gown
Of white silk wrapped round him. He nods and sighs.

I know I see like this because I use
A heritage of seeing to direct
All shapes into a schematic pattern.

I know that man's great task is to unlearn
These modes of seeing, that he must expect
The unexpected. But what does he lose?

Alan Bold

1. What connection is there between the rhyme scheme and the division of the sonnet into verses?
2. Where does the main division come in the poem?
3. What is *an aged pundit*?
4. Remembering that a nebula is 'a luminous patch made by a cluster of distant stars', what, therefore, would give the impression of *a gown of white silk*?
5. Alan Bold says in the poem: *I know I see like this because* . . . Say briefly how he does see the Trifid Nebula.
6. Why does he see the Nebula this way?
7. What does he say is unsatisfactory about seeing the Nebula in this way?
8. Answer the question at the end of the poem: what does he lose?

After dark vapours have oppress'd our plains

After dark vapours have oppress'd our plains
For a long dreary season, comes a day
Born of the gentle South, and clears away
From the sick heavens all unseemly stains.
The anxious month, relieved from its pains,
Takes as a long-lost right the feel of May,
The eye-lids with the passing coolness play,
Like rose-leaves with the drip of summer rains.
And calmest thoughts come round us — as of leaves
Budding — fruit ripening in stillness — autumn suns
Smiling at eve upon the quiet sheaves, —
Sweet Sappho's cheek, — a sleeping infant's breath, —
The gradual sand that through an hour-glass runs, —
A woodland rivulet, — a Poet's death.

John Keats

1. Which words and phrases suggest that the opening lines are to be taken metaphorically as a description of an illness that has just passed?
2. What is a *plain* in the ordinary sense? What is Keats referring to when he applies this word to himself?
3. What mood has come over Keats since the *dark vapours* passed?
4. Which particular words in the similes in the sestet help to create this mood?
5. What do the phrases suggest about the things that gave Keats pleasure? (Sappho was a Greek poetess)
6. The final phrase — *a Poet's death* — comes unexpectedly after the images of quietness. Is Keats referring to himself? What does the phrase reveal about Keats's attitude to death?
7. Can you reconcile this attitude with the fact that he is relieved to have survived a long period of illness?
8. Does the style of the poem suggest an ease and relaxation in its composition?

Sonnet 104

To me, fair friend, you never can be old;
For as you were when first your eye I eyed,
Such seems your beauty still. Three winters cold
Have from the forests shook three summers' pride;
Three beauteous springs to yellow autumn turn'd
In process of the seasons have I seen,
Three April perfumes in three hot Junes burn'd,
Since first I saw you fresh, which yet are green.
Ah! yet doth beauty, like a dial-hand,
Steal from his figure, and no pace perceived,
So your sweet hue, which methinks still doth stand,
Hath motion, and mine eye may be deceived.
For fear of which, hear this, thou age unbred:
Ere you were born was beauty's summer dead.

William Shakespeare

1. Where do the divisions of thought occur within the fourteen lines?
2. What is the first main thought expressed in the poem?
3. What does Shakespeare mean by the following phrases?
   summers' pride   *yellow autumn*   *April perfumes*
4. In what sense is the word *green* used in line 8?

5. The line ending: *Three winters cold* until the line ending: *hot Junes burned* means simply three years. Can you justify Shakespeare's way of expressing this fact?
6. What is of interest in the phrase *eye I eyed?* What literal phrase could be substituted to convey the same meaning? Would it be better or worse than the original?
7. What is *which* referring to in the phrase (line 13): *for fear of which?*
8. In the last line of the sonnet, what is *you* referring to? Who is *beauty's summer?*
9. In your opinion, is the idea expressed in the sonnet a sentimental or a realistic one?

The Hill

Where are Elmer, Herman, Bert, Tom and Charley,
The weak of will, the strong of arm, the clown, the boozer, the fighter?
All, all, are sleeping on the hill.

One passed in a fever,
One was burned in a mine,
One was killed in a brawl,
One died in a jail,
One fell from a bridge toiling for children and wife —
All, all are sleeping, sleeping, sleeping on the hill.

Where are Ella, Kate, Mag, Lizzie and Edith,
The tender heart, the simple soul, the loud, the proud, the happy one? —
All, all, are sleeping on the hill.

One died in shameful child-birth,
One of a thwarted love,
One at the hands of a brute in a brothel,
One of a broken pride, in the search for heart's desire,
One after life in far-away London and Paris
Was brought to her little space by Ella and Kate and Mag —
All, all are sleeping, sleeping, sleeping on the hill.

Where are Uncle Isaac and Aunt Emily,
And old Towny Kincaid and Sevigne Houghton,
And Major Walker who had talked
With venerable men of the revolution? —
All, all, are sleeping on the hill.

They brought them dead sons from the war,
And daughters whom life had crushed,
And their children fatherless, crying —
All, all are sleeping, sleeping, sleeping on the hill.

Where is Old Fiddler Jones
Who played with life all his ninety years,
Braving the sleet with bared breast,
Drinking, rioting, thinking neither of wife nor kin,
Nor gold, nor love, nor heaven?

Lo! he babbles of the fish-frys of long ago,
Of the horse-races of long ago at Clary's Grove,
Of what Abe Lincoln said
One time at Springfield.

Edgar Lee Masters

1. The poem is written in free verse and is without rhyme or metrical regularity; yet there is a recognisable structure to it. Can you say what this is by tracing the development of the subject of the poem?
2. Much of the poetic effect is achieved by the use of rhythm and repetition. Give some examples to show how the poet has done this.
3. Why do you think the poet makes no attempt to continue the rhythmical effect into the last verse of the poem?
4. What seems to be common to all the characters who are sleeping on the hill?
5. What key phrase defines Old Fiddler Jones's attitude towards life?
6. Comparing Old Fiddler Jones with the other characters in the poem, what conclusion do you think is being suggested by Edgar Lee Masters?
7. What do you like, or dislike, about this poem?

Visiting Hour

The hospital smell
combs my nostrils
as they go bobbing along
green and yellow corridors.

What seems a corpse
is trundled into a lift and vanishes
heavenward.

I will not feel, I will not
feel, until
I have to.

Nurses walk lightly, swiftly,
here and up and down and there,
their slender waists miraculously
carrying their burden
of so much pain, so
many deaths, their eyes
still clear after
so many farewells.

Ward 7. She lies
in a white cave of forgetfulness.
A withered hand
trembles on its stalk. Eyes move
behind eyelids too heavy
to raise. Into an arm wasted
of colour a glass fang is fixed,
not guzzling but giving.
And between her and me
distance shrinks till there is none left
but the distance of pain that neither she nor I
can cross.

She smiles a little at this
black figure in her white cave
who clumsily rises
in the round swimming waves of a bell
and dizzily goes off, growing fainter,
not smaller, leaving behind only
books that will not be read
and fruitless fruit.

Norman MacCaig

1. What advantages are there in using free verse for the form of
    this poem?
2. Norman MacCaig says:

    I will not feel, I will not
    feel, until
    I have to.

    What feelings is he referring to? Where in the poem does he
    treat a serious incident humorously in order to avoid these
    feelings?

3. How does his admiration of the nurses suggest what he himself is reluctant to experience?
4. What details convey the age and the illness of the woman he is visiting?
5. Why, when he left, was he *growing fainter, not smaller?*
6. How are we made to feel that the visit has been a futile one?
7. Is the style of the poem obviously *poetic*, or is it that of natural speech? Or is it a combination of both? Quote examples in your answer.
8. Sum up what visiting hour at a hospital meant for Norman MacCaig.

The Song of Wandering Aengus

I went out to the hazel wood,
    Because a fire was in my head,
And cut and peeled a hazel wand,
And hooked a berry to a thread:
And when white moths were on the wing,
    And moth-like stars were flickering out,
I dropped the berry in a stream
    And caught a little silver trout.

When I had laid it on the floor
    I went to blow the fire a-flame,
But something rustled on the floor,
And someone called me by my name:
It had become a glimmering girl
    With apple blossom in her hair
Who called me by my name and ran
    And faded through the brightening air.

Though I am old with wandering
    Through hollow lands and hilly lands,
I will find out where she has gone,
    And kiss her lips and take her hands:
And walk among long dappled grass,
And pluck till time and tides are done
The silver apples of the moon,
    The golden apples of the sun.

W B Yeats

The Hero
(After *The Song of Wandering Aengus* by W B Yeats)

I went out to the city streets,
Because a fire was in my head,
And saw the people passing by,
And wished the youngest of them dead,
And twisted by a bitter past,
And poisoned by a cold despair,
I found at last a resting-place
And left my hatred ticking there.

When I was fleeing from the night
And sweating in my room again,
I heard the old futilities
Exploding like a cry of pain;
But horror, should it touch the heart,
Would freeze my hand upon the fuse,
And I must shed no tears for those
Who merely have a life to lose.

Though I am sick with murdering,
Though killing is my native land,
I will find out where death has gone,
And kiss his lips and take his hand;
And hide among the withered grass,
And pluck, till love and life are done,
The shrivelled apples of the moon,
The cankered apples of the sun.

Roger Woddis

The Hero is a serious parody, not aimed at making fun of the
original, but at showing a contrast between the romantic youth
searching for love and the fanatical youth intent on killing.
1. What similarities are there in structure and phrasing in the two
    poems?
2. Which lines bring out the contrast most starkly?
3. How does the *fire in the head* differ in the two youths?
4. In what way can one poem be said to be mystical and the
    other realistic?
5. What point is added to *The Hero* by knowing the poem on
    which it is based?
6. What significance do you see in the title, *The Hero*?
7. Which of these poems do you prefer? Or do you see both as
    having some quality and interest? Give reasons for your
    answer.

Hamnavoe Market

They drove to the Market with ringing pockets.

Folster found a girl
Who put wounds on his face and throat,
Small and diagonal, like red doves.

Johnston stood beside the barrel.
All day he stood there.
He woke in a ditch, his mouth full of ashes.

Grieve bought a balloon and a goldfish.
He swung through the air.
He fired shotguns, rolled pennies, ate sweet fog from a stick.

Heddle was at the Market also.
I know nothing of his activities.
He is and always was a quiet man.

Garson fought three rounds with a negro boxer,
And received thirty shillings,
Much applause, and an eye loaded with thunder.

Where did they find Flett?
They found him in a brazen circle,
All flame and blood, a new Salvationist.

A gypsy saw in the hand of Halcro
Great strolling herds, harvests, a proud woman.
He wintered in the poorhouse.

They drove home from the Market under the stars
Except for Johnston
Who lay in a ditch, his mouth full of dying fires.

George Mackay Brown

1. Without mentioning any names, say briefly what the subject of the poem is.
2. Explain what structure George Mackay Brown has used for his poem.
3. What do you understand by the following metaphors?
   i) *with ringing pockets;*
   ii) *wounds on his face and throat;*
   iii) *his mouth full of ashes;*
   iv) *sweet fog from a stick;*
   v) *an eye loaded with thunder;*
   vi) *in a brazen circle, all flame and blood.*

4. Can you see anything particularly appropriate in the simile *like red doves?*
5. Which character is described in absolutely literal terms?
6. Why would Halcro have been disappointed that he wintered in the poor house?
7. What contrasts of character has George Mackay Brown got into his poem?
8. Imagine that a group of assorted characters — including, perhaps, some of your acquaintance — is going on a day's outing to a football match, a race meeting, a pop festival, a fair, a seaside resort, or something similar. Write a short stanza on each of the characters, describing what he, or she, got up to on that day.

The Storm

What blinding storm there was! How it
Flashed with a leap and lance of nails,
    Lurching, O suddenly
    Over the lambing hills,

Hounding me there! With sobbing lungs
I reeled past kirk and alehouse
    And the thousand candles
    Of gorse round my mother's yard,

And down the sand shot out my skiff
Into the long green jaws, while deep
    In summer's sultry throat
    Dry thunder stammered.

Swiftly the sail drew me over
The snarling Sound, scudding before
    The heraldic clouds now
    Rampant all around.

The sea — organ and harps — wailed miserere;
Swung me in fluent valleys, poised
    On icy yielding peaks
    Hissing spume, until

Rousay before me, the stout mast
Snapped, billowing down helpless sail.
    What evil joy the storm
    Seized us! plunged and spun!

And flung us, skiff and man (wave-crossed, God-lost)
On a rasp of rock! . . . The shore breakers,
    Stained chancel lights,
    Cluster of mellow bells,

Crossed hands, scent of holy water . . .
The storm danced over all that night,
    Loud with demons, but I
    Safe in Brother Colm's cell.

Next morning in tranced sunshine
The corn lay squashed on every hill;
    Tang and tern were strewn
    Among highest pastures.

I tell you this, my son: after
That Godsent storm, I find peace here
    These many years with
    The Gray Monks of Eynhallow.

George Mackay Brown

1. Consider the subject of the poem: the narrator is caught in a
   storm; he staggers past the church (*kirk*), the alehouse and his
   mother's yard to a sandy beach where he sets sail in his small
   skiff for the island of Rousay in the Orkneys. The storm gets
   worse, the mast breaks, the sail hurtles down, the skiff capsizes
   and is dashed against the rocks . . . What are we told in the
   remainder of the poem?
2. The style is rich in figurative language, giving the poem a great
   deal of vitality and animation. a) Trace the personification
   throughout the poem. b) Say what visual link the poet is
   establishing in the metaphors: *candles of gorse; heraldic
   clouds; tranced sunshine.* What sound is suggested in: *the sea —
   organ and harps —?* What sensation of touch is implied in: *a
   rasp of rock?*
3. Study the form of the poem. What regularity is there in the
   structure of the verses? Is there any regular metre or rhyme?
   What rhyming effect is created in: *wave-crossed, God-lost;
   plunged . . . spun . . . flung; mellow bells?*
4. The poet makes considerable use of alliteration, both for
   emphasis and for rhythmic effect. Quote some examples.
5. Which words in verse five are onomatopoeic?
6. Is there anything in the poem which might suggest that the
   storm represents a spiritual experience?
7. What impression has the poem made on you? Comment on the
   subject and on the effectiveness of the poetic technique.

ygUDuh

ydoan
yunnuhstan

ydoan o
yunnuhstan dem
yguduh ged

yunnuhstan dem doidee
yguduh ged riduh
ydoan o nudn
LISN bud LISN

dem
gud
am

lidl yelluh bas
tuds weer goin

duhSIVILEYEzum

E E Cummings

1. Translate the poem.
2. What is E E Cummings attempting to do through the diction of the poem?
3. What reasons are there for giving the poem its unusual shape or form?
4. What use is made of capital letters in the poem?
5. What point is E E Cummings making?
6. How successful has he been?

Where's the Poet?

Where's the Poet? show him! show him,
Muses nine! that I may know him.
'Tis the man who with a man
Is an equal, be he King,
Or poorest of the beggar-clan,
Or any other wondrous thing
A man may be 'twixt ape and Plato;
'Tis the man who with a bird,
Wren, or eagle, finds his way to
All its instincts; he hath heard
The lion's roaring, and can tell

What his horny throat expresseth,
And to him the tiger's yell
Comes articulate and presseth
On his ear like mother-tongue.

John Keats

1. What does Keats make the essential characteristic of a poet?
2. Which poets, in your opinion, live up to Keats's definition?
   Choose one poem dealing with a bird or an animal and another
   poem dealing with a human character and show to what extent
   the poet has been able to enter imaginatively into the life of
   his subject — to *find his way to all its instincts* — and to bring
   it alive for the reader.

Write on the following poems, commenting on what in them seems
to you to be of particular significance. You should consider them
under the following headings: i) subject; ii) form; iii) style;
iv) final impression.

i)   What is the poet saying in his poem? Is he presenting a
     description, an experience from life, an idea, a narrative? What
     attitude has he to his subject? Give a brief outline of the
     poem.
ii) What form of verse has the poet used? Has he used the form
     skilfully and has it helped him in the expression of his subject?
     What use is made of metre, rhyme, rhythm, alliteration? Do
     they contribute to the artistic effect of the poem?
iii) What style of language is used? Is it simple, literal and direct,
     colloquial, figurative, imaginative, classical? Comment on the
     use of metaphor, simile, personification, symbol and any
     special effects the poet has created.
iv) What is the poem's most striking characteristic? Why was the
     poem written? Has it given you pleasure, helped you to a new
     understanding, created a strong impression on you? Or has it
     met with little response? What is wrong with it? Sum up what
     the poet was attempting to do and how well he has done it.

To a Young Poet

For the first twenty years you are still growing,
Bodily, that is; as a poet, of course,
You are not born yet. It's the next ten
You cut your teeth on to emerge smirking

For your brash courtship of the muse.
You will take seriously those first affairs
With young poems, but no attachments
Formed then but come to shame you,
When love has changed to a grave service
Of a cold queen.
              From forty on
You learn from the sharp cuts and jags
Of poems that have come to pieces
In your crude hands how to assemble
With more skill the arbitrary parts
Of ode or sonnet, while time fosters
A new impulse to conceal your wounds
From her and from a bold public,
Given to pry.
              You are old now
As years reckon, but in that slower
World of the poet you are just coming
To sad manhood, knowing the smile
Of her proud face is not for you.

R S Thomas

The following lines are from the Anglo-Saxon epic, *Beowulf*, which describes how the hero Beowulf destroyed the monster, Grendel, who was terrorising the court of the Danish king, Hrothgar. Scyld Scefing was the legendary founder of the Danish nation. As a child he had arrived mysteriously from over the sea and he lived to unite the Danish tribes and to become their king. *Beowulf* opens with this description of his sea-burial.

At the hour shaped for him Scyld departed,
the many-strengthed moved into his Master's keeping.

They carried him out to the current sea,
his sworn arms-fellows, as he himself had asked
while he wielded by his words, Ward of the Scyldings,
beloved folk-founder; long had he ruled.

A boat with a ringed neck rode in the haven,
icy, out-eager, the aetheling's vessel,
and there they laid out their lord and master,
dealer of wound gold, in the waist of the ship,
in majesty by the mast.
              A mound of treasures
from far countries was fetched aboard her,

and it is said that no boat was ever more bravely fitted out
with the weapons of a warrior, war accoutrement,
bill and byrnies; on his breast were set
treasures and trappings to travel with him
on his far faring into the flood's sway.

This hoard was not less great than the gifts he had
from those who sent him, on the sill of life,
over seas, alone, a small child.

High over head they hoisted and fixed
a gold signum; gave him to the flood,
let the seas take him, with sour hearts
and mourning moods. Men have not the knowledge
to say with any truth — however tall beneath the heavens,
however much listened to — who unloaded that boat.

The Blue Jay

The blue jay with a crest on his head
Comes round the cabin in the snow.
He runs in the snow like a bit of blue metal,
Turning his back on everything.

From the pine-tree that towers and hisses like a pillar of
        shaggy cloud
Immense above the cabin
Comes a strident laugh as we approach, this little black dog
        and I.
So halts the little black bitch on four spread paws in the
        snow
And looks up inquiringly into the pillar of cloud,
With a tinge of misgiving.

Ca-a-a! comes the scrape of ridicule out of the tree.

What voice of the Lord is that, from the tree of smoke?

Oh, Bibbles, little black bitch in the snow,
With a pinch of snow in the groove of your silly snub nose,
What do you look at *me* for?
What do you look at me for, with such misgiving?

It's the blue jay laughing at us,
It's the blue jay jeering at us, Bibs.

Every day since the snow is here
The blue jay paces round the cabin, very busy, picking up
    bits,
Turning his back on us all,
And bobbing his thick dark crest about the snow, as if darkly
    saying:
I ignore those folk who look out.

You acid-blue metallic bird,
You thick bird with a strong crest,
Who are you?
Whose boss are you, with all your bully ways?
You copper-sulphate blue bird!

                                            D H Lawrence

Starlings

Can you keep it so,
cool tree, making a blue cage
for an obstreperous population? —
for a congregation of mediaeval scholars
quarrelling in several languages? —
for busybodies marketing
in the bazaar of green leaves? —
for clockwork fossils that can't be still even
when the Spring runs down?
No tree, no blue cage can contain
that restlessness. They whirr off
and sow themselves in a scattered handful
on the grass — and are
bustling monks
tilling their green precincts.

                                            Norman MacCaig

A Square Dance

In Flanders fields in Northern France
They're all doing a brand new dance
It makes you happy and out of breath
And it's called the Dance of Death

Everybody stands in line
Everybody's feeling fine
We're all going to a hop
1 — 2 — 3 and over the top

It's the dance designed to thrill
It's the mustard gas quadrille
A dance for men — girls have no say in it
For your partner is a bayonet

See how the dancers sway and run
To the rhythm of the gun
Swing your partner dos-y-doed
All around the shells explode

Honour your partner form a square
Smell the burning in the air
Over the barbed wire kicking high
Men like shirts hung out to dry

If you fall that's no disgrace
Someone else will take your place
'Old soldiers never die . . . '
. . . Only young ones

In Flanders fields where mortars blaze
They're all doing the latest craze
Khaki dancers out of breath
Doing the glorious Dance of Death
Doing the glorious (clap, clap) Dance of Death.

Roger McGough

A LIST OF POETICAL TERMS

Accent Another name for stress in a line of verse; an accented syllable is a stressed one.

Allusion A reference to something real or fictitious outside the poem. A **classical allusion** is a reference to Greek or Roman characters or events. *Sweet Sappho's cheek* (Keats); *That Orpheus self may heave his head / From golden slumber on a bed / Of heaped Elysian flowers* (Milton).

Anticlimax A disappointing collapse — when the anticipated excitement is replaced by something mild or comically inappropriate.

Antithesis A balance of opposite statements in a line of poetry or in a couplet: *With mirth in funeral, and with dirge in marriage* (Hamlet); *In wit a man; simplicity a child* (Pope's epitaph on Gray). See the quotation from Pope, page 68.

Apostrophe When a person (or a personification) is addressed directly in a poem: *O Wild West Wind* (Shelley); *Busy old fool, unruly Sun* (Donne); *Hail, bounteous May.* (Milton).

Archaism (adj. archaic) A word that is no longer commonly used in speech or in writing; an out-of-date word. Examples: *methinks, sirrah, lea, mead, o'er, thou, morn.*

Ballad metre See chapter on Metre.

Bard Celtic poet in pre-feudal England who composed and sang songs to gatherings of nobles and warriors.

Climax The point of greatest interest or excitement which has been led up to by a graded series of events. In *Edward, Edward* (page 57) the admission by Edward of the murder is the first climax; the second climax is when he reveals that his mother advised him to do it.

Conceit An intricate or clever metaphor — often developed at length — which tends to surprise or amuse the reader. It can show real insight, or, taken to an extreme, can appear contrived and insincere. Many Elizabethan sonnets were based on conceits. *My mistress' eyes are nothing like the sun* (Shakespeare). Donne's poem *The Flea* contains a brilliant conceit.

Diction Choice of words and phrases; the vocabulary a poet uses

128

to create style and effect in a poem. Diction can be, for instance, colloquial, archaic, classical, plain, ornate, literary, technical, Biblical, contemporary. Examples taken from poems in the book are:

Archaic: *Go, Lovely Rose!* (page 42): *thee, fair, shuns, graces spied, hadst, abide, uncommended, forth, suffer, wondrous.*

Original (making use of rare or invented words): *Inversnaid* (page 49): *darksome, rollrock, flutes, windpuff, twindles, fell-frowning, degged, beadbonny.*

Colloquial American: *Jazz Fantasia* (page 53): *batter, cool, jazzmen, sling, tin pans, lonesome, like you wanted somebody terrible, cop, clinch, can the rough stuff.*

Classical: from *Paradise Lost* (page 65): *clime, seat, celestial, sovereign, dispose, supreme, infernal, profoundest, possessor, Almighty.*

Simple, conversational: *Who's Who* (page 74): *all the facts, how he ran away, weep his pints, little jobs about the house, potter round the garden.*

Doggerel Weak verse that relies on a repetitive rhythm and obvious rhymes for its effect. Dr Johnson caricatured it in: *As with my hat upon my head / I walked along the Strand, / I there did meet another man / With his hat in his hand.*

Elegy A poem of melancholy reflection: Gray's *Elegy Written in a Country Churchyard.*

Elision The omission of a letter for rhythmic effect, usually indicated by an apostrophe: *o'er, awa', ne'er.*

Epic A long narrative poem dealing with events on a grand scale, often with a hero whose qualities and exploits place him above the average human. Homer's *Iliad;* Milton's *Paradise Lost.*

Epitaph An inscription on a tomb, commemorating the dead person's life and character. On the tomb of Sir Thomas Wyatt (of sonnet fame) in Sherborne Abbey there is the epitaph: *Wyatt resteth here, that quick could never rest.*

Form In poetry this can refer to i) the type of composition, such as epic, lyric, narrative; or ii) the structure of the verse — the stanzaic pattern, the metre, the rhyme, which in turn, determine whether the form of the poem is ballad, sonnet, blank verse, free verse, etc.

Half-rhyme Another term for **consonance** (see chapter on Rhyme): when the consonants following the main vowel rhyme, but the vowels themselves do not rhyme: *grope-cup, drunkard-conquered*. Note that it differs from **pararhyme**, in which the consonants before and after the vowel are rhymed.

Hyperbole A poetic exaggeration, used to convey intense emotion; not intended to be taken literally. *All the perfumes of Arabia will not sweeten this little hand* (Macbeth); *I lov'd Ophelia; forty thousand brothers / Could not, with all their quantity of love, / Make up my sum.* (Hamlet). *She is all states, and all princes, I / Nothing else is.* (Donne).

Imagery Most simply, imagery is 'a picture made out of words' (C Day Lewis). It need not necessarily be metaphorical; it usually appeals to one of the five senses. *What blinding storm there was; thousand candles of gorse; cluster of mellow bells* (George Mackay Brown). An abstract phrase is not an image: *I find peace here.*

Irony There are many forms of irony. In poetry, one of the most common is verbal irony, when what is said is understood to mean its opposite. When Mark Antony refers to Brutus and the assassins of Caesar as *all honourable men* he is ironically implying that they are anything but honourable men. *Hi!* by Walter de la Mare is an ironical poem:

> Hi! handsome hunting man,
> Fire your little gun.
> Bang! Now the animal
> Is dead and dumb and done.
> Never to peep again, creep again, leap again,
> Eat or sleep or drink again, Oh, what fun!

Lay A song or a medieval tale of love and adventure.

Lyric Originally a poem to be sung to a lyre; now a short poem expressing a mood or a feeling, characterised by its light, rhythmical structure.

Mixed metaphor Two or more metaphors combined or juxtaposed, sometimes with ludicrous results, as in Thisby's lament over Pyramus: *These lily brows, / This cherry nose, / These yellow cowslip cheeks;* but common enough, especially in Shakespeare, without causing hilarity: *And I, of ladies most deject and wretched / That suck'd the honey of his music vows.* (Ophelia).

Mood The atmosphere created in the poem itself (as distinct from the **tone**, which is the poet's attitude to his subject). The mood of *Discord in Childhood* (page 111) is heavy, oppressive, violent, but the tone (of the poet) is calm, almost detached, but touched with sadness and regret. *Among Ourselves* (page 40) depicts a mood of boredom and suppressed irritation. In *The Hill* (page 114) the mood changes from tragic and melancholic to buoyant and comic. In *Counting the Beats* (page 101) the mood is secretive, oppressively romantic, whilst Graves's tone is ironical.

Octosyllabic couplet Two rhymed lines, each consisting of eight syllables and four stresses.

Ode Originally a song in honour of gods and heroes; now a formal ceremonious lyric, characterised by strong passion.

Ottava Rima A stanza of eight iambic lines, rhyming abababcc. It is most successfully used in English poetry by Byron in *Don Juan* where the epigrammatic climax in the final couplet is particularly effective.

Paradox A statement which seems at first to be self-contradictory, but which on closer inspection turns out to have a valid meaning. *Beware the fury of a patient man* (Dryden); *dark with excessive light* (Milton); *We shall not cease from exploration / And the end of all our exploring / Will be to arrive where we started / And know the place for the first time.* (Eliot).

Pastoral verse Poetry dealing with country life, which is treated in a romantic, non-realistic way; shepherds and shepherdesses figure prominently; the classical setting was usually Arcadia, a peaceful mountain district of Greece.

Pathetic fallacy A phrase coined by John Ruskin describing the tendency of poets and painters to ascribe to natural objects the feelings of human beings: *the cruel, crawling foam* (Kingsley). Ruskin was, therefore, objecting to personification, but more specifically to its being used sentimentally or morbidly by poets.

Poetic diction Used in two senses: i) artificial and ornate language, commonly used by poets in the eighteenth century and against which Wordsworth protested in the preface to the Lyrical Ballads: *Awake, AEolian lyre, awake,/And give to rapture all thy trembling strings* (Gray); and ii) the imaginative and impassioned language of poetry. To distinguish between the two uses it is best to refer to the former as 'artifical' poetic diction.

Prosody The study of the principles of verse structure, including metre, rhyme, rhythm and stanza form.

Pun The use of a word to suggest two separate meanings at the same time. Used for comic effect: *Ben Battle was a soldier bold, /*

And used to wars' alarms; / But a cannon ball took off his legs, /
So he laid down his arms. (Hood). It can also be used seriously, as
when Lady Macbeth says: *If he do bleed, / I'll gild the faces of the*
grooms withal, / For it must seem their guilt.

Quatrain A stanza of four lines, rhymed or unrhymed. The most
common of all stanza forms in European poetry and used
especially in ballads.

Quantitative verse Greek and Latin metre was based, not on the
number of stresses in a line, as English verse is, but upon the
'quantities' of syllables — that is, the length of time taken to say
them. A long syllable was regarded as equivalent in time value to
two short syllables.

Refrain A word, phrase, line or lines repeated (often with small
variations) at intervals throughout a poem, usually at the end of a
stanza. It may stress the spirit of the poem ('With a hey, and a ho,
and a hey nonino'), or emphasise a significant aspect of the story
or theme. A refrain establishes a rhythm, marks off metrical units
and can be used for comic or dramatic effect. *Edward, Edward*
(page 57): *Edward, Edward; Mother, Mother; The Hill* (page 114):
All, all are sleeping on the hill; The Old Gumbie Cat (page 12):
She sits and sits and sits and sits — and that's what makes a
Gumbie Cat; Boots (page 54): *There's no discharge in the war.*

Rhyme Royal A seven-line stanza of iambic pentameter, rhyming
ababbcc. Called 'royal' because James I of Scotland used it.

Spenserian stanza A nine-line stanza, rhyming ababbcbcc, named
after Edmund Spenser, the Elizabethan poet who originated it.
The first eight lines are iambic pentameter, the last line is an
Alexandrine and contains six stresses.

Sprung rhythm A term coined by Gerard Manley Hopkins in
which a metrical foot consists of a single stress or a single stress
plus any number of unstressed syllables — thus differing from the
normal metrical foot, which consists of a stressed syllable plus
either one or two unstressed syllables. The single stresses in sprung
rhythm often followed one another without intervening unstressed
syllables. It is a form of pure stress verse.

Terza Rima A verse form composed of iambic tercets, rhyming
aba bcb cdc, etc., the rhyme forming a link between the stanzas.
Used by Shelley in *Ode to the West Wind.*

Tone The poet's attitude towards his subjects — possibly
humorous, satirical, sentimental, cynical, bitter, dispassionate,

reverent, serious, ironical. Examples from poems in the book: *Morte d'Arthur* (page 106): solemn, befitting the subject; *Skylarks* (page 107): wonder, admiration; *The Last Laugh* (page 110): bitter and disillusioned; *After dark vapours* (page 112): optimistic, full of hope; *Futility* (page 18): gentle, becoming bitter and enraged; *The Burial of Sir John Moore* (page 90): reverent, solemn, melancholy; *Not a Sous Has He Got* (page 91): satirical, irreverent.

Triplet (or tercet) A verse unit of three lines, usually containing rhyme.

Trope A figure of speech, such as personification, metaphor, etc.

THEMES IN THE POEMS

GENERAL QUESTIONS

1. Describe the outlook of the lovers written about in each of the following poems and say how each differs from the others: *Counting the Beats; Go, lovely Rose!; Young Hunting.* Which poem do you prefer?

2. Which of the poems dealing with the relationship between a man and a woman do you find yourself most in sympathy with? Give an account of the poem and say why you find it better than other poems on the same subject.

3. In *Where's the Poet?* Keats claims that a poet ought to be able to enter imaginatively into the life of a man (beggar or king), a beast or a bird and reveal its true nature. Which poets seem to you to have done this? Choose any three poems to show how a poet has revealed a deep understanding of his subject and brought it alive for his reader.

4. Choose three poems which illustrate a wide range of human character. Show how the poet presents the character and what attitude, if any, he adopts towards it.

5. Poems can present ideas to a reader. Show how any three poets have presented their ideas in poetic form and say what you think of their ideas.

6. Which poems would you criticise as being deficient in what you yourself consider to be true poetic quality? Explain what the poet was aiming at in writing the poem and then add your own critical commentary.

7. What contrasting attitudes to death in war are presented in the following poems? *Futility; The Burial of Sir John Moore at Corunna; A Square Dance.*

8. Choose any three poems which have: *a*) given you pleasure to read; or *b*) taught you something; or *c*) defeated your understanding. Give a short account of the poems and explain your reaction to them.

9. Do you prefer twentieth-century poetry to poetry from a previous century, or vice versa? Choose three poems from the period you prefer and say why they appeal to you more than the poems from the other period.

10. In which poems do you think the poet reveals himself most openly and honestly? Choose three poems to illustrate your answer and say what impression the poet gives of himself.

11. What are the advantages of free verse as a poetic form? Choose two or three poems to illustrate the characteristics of free

verse and show what the poet has gained by choosing this verse
form.
12. Discuss some of the more unorthodox and experimental
    poetry in this book. Does this style of poetry appeal to you, or
    do you prefer traditional forms?
13. Explain what qualities you have found in any one verse form
    by referring to three or four examples.
14. Which poets seem to you to be greatly interested in figurative
    language and which seem to write plain statements? Compare
    three or four poems written in contrasting styles of language
    and say which you prefer.
15. Illustrate the appeal of *a)* the limerick and *b)* the haiku by
    analysing the subjects and the styles of these two poetic forms.
16. Write an appreciation and criticism of the poems in this book
    by one of the following poets: Ted Hughes, R S Thomas,
    D H Lawrence, Wilfred Owen, William Shakespeare.
17. Choose three poems that contain a dramatic situation. Show
    how the poet builds up the situation — perhaps through the
    characters — and explain how the drama is resolved.
18. Write an appreciation of two poems that might be classed as
    'light' or humorous verse.
19. Is it necessary, or desirable, to be able to recognise the poet's
    technique in order to appreciate his poem? Or should a poem
    be read simply for enjoyment? Argue for or against the study
    of technique in poetry.
20. What would be lost to culture and civilisation if the art of
    poetry did not exist?

INDEX OF POETS